A Good And Favorable Wind

The Unusual Story Of A Submarine Under Sail And Its Cautionary Lessons For The Modern Navy

David L. Johnston & Ric Hedman

With Illustrations By Jim Christley

Nimble Books LLC

Copyright © 2022 David L. Johnston & Ric Hedman

Illustrations © 2022 Jim Christley

All rights reserved.

ISBNs:
- 9781608882007 (hc)
- 9781608881970 (pb)
- 9781608881987 (Kindle)

This book is composed in Adobe Skolar (body) and Proxima Nova (headings). The cover is Rockwell.

CONTENTS

Figures v
Tables vii
Foreword ix
Preface xi
About the Authors xiii
    David Johnston xiii
    Ric Hedman xiv
Authors' Notes & Acknowledgements xvi
    Dave xvi
    Ric xvii
Abbreviations xix
Publisher's Note xxi
Part 1 1
    Monday, 02 May 1921, 8:00 A.M. 1
        11:00 A.M. Emergency Orders And Hurried Preparations 14
        12:00 Noon. Provisions And Fuel 19
        4:50 P.M. Underway For The Search 24
    The Next Nine Days 33
    Wednesday, 11 May 1921, 140 Miles Southeast Of Hawaii 47
    11 May 1921, 9:15 P.M. "Hoist With Our Own Petard" 49
    Night of 11-12 May 1921, Adrift 52
    12 May 1921, Rigging Sails 56
    12-15 May 1921, Underway On Wind Power 59
    15-17 May 1921, Arrival At Hilo And Return To Pearl Harbor 65
Part 2 71
    17-31 May 1921, Submarine Base Pearl Harbor, T.H. 73
    How And Why 80
        Logs 82
        Procedural Compliance 83

>   Blowing The Tanks 85
>   Fuel Tank Leak 85
>   Leadership, Oversight, And Organizational Issues 87
> The Aftermath 93
> Lessons Learned 99
> Postscript: The Fate of the USS *Conestoga* (AT-54) 102
> Appendix A. Sailing List, USS *R-14* (SS-91), May 1921 107
> Appendix B. A Short History of PigBoats.COM 109
> Bibliography 110
>   Official U.S. Navy Documents 110
>   Books 110
>   Magazine Articles and Monographs 110
>   Newspaper Articles 110
> Index 111

FIGURES

Figure 1. DCC(SS/SW) David L. Johnston, USN (Ret.) xiii
Figure 2. TN(SS) Richard C. Hedman, USN xiv
Figure 3. Midshipman Alexander Dean Douglas as a cadet at the U.S. Naval Academy, 1917. 5
Figure 4. Lieutenant Vincent A. Clarke, Jr., the *R-14*'s official Commanding Officer in May 1921. n. 6
Figure 5. Electrician 2c Valoris E. Field on the *R-14*'s forward deck near the deck gun. 7
Figure 6. Chief Gunner's Mate (Torpedo) Harry Woodworth, USN. 8
Figure 7. Gunners Mate 1c John J. Dorsey and Gunners Mate 1c Winfield E. Bridges, members of the *R-14*'s crew during the sailing incident. 9
Figure 8. Naval Station and the Navy Yard Pearl Harbor, summer 1919. 10
Figure 9. Submarine Base Pearl Harbor, June 1921. 11
Figure 10. *R-20* and *R-12* alongside at Honolulu, circa 1920. 12
Figure 11. Illustration by Jim Christley of the Electric Boat design for the R-class submarines, as built. 13
Figure 12. USS *Conestoga* (AT-54). 17
Figure 13. The *USS Eagle No. 58* (PE-58), a sister boat to the *Eagle No. 14* that Chester Nimitz used as his flagship for the search operation. T 18
Figure 14. *R-14* outbound in the main channel of Pearl Harbor, early 1920's. .. 22
Figure 15. Fuel Pier, Naval Station Pearl Harbor, mid 1920s. 23
Figure 16. Ensign Roy Trent Gallemore early in his career, on the forecastle of the USS *Des Moines* (Cruiser #15), circa 1919. Photo courtesy of Katie Gallemore Eliot. 28
Figure 17. The bridge of the *R-14*, circa 1921. 29
Figure 18. The voyage of the *R-14*, 02-17 May 1921. 30
Figure 19. The forward battery compartment of the *R-16*, representative of the *R-14*. 31
Figure 20. The forward battery compartment of *R-16*, looking aft and to port. 32

Figure 21. The after battery compartment of the *R-16*, looking forward and to starboard. 37

Figure 22. The boat's diving control station, port side of the control room. 38

Figure 23. The boat's electrical speed controls, located on the aft bulkhead in the control room. 39

Figure 24. The control room of the *R-16*, again representative of the R-class. 40

Figure 25. Kingston valve control levers, aft starboard corner of the control room. 41

Figure 26. Photo taken aboard the *R-14*, showing the ballast control manifold, forward starboard corner of the control room. 42

Figure 27. The aft port corner of the after battery compartment on *R-16*, showing the boat's galley. 43

Figure 28. The after battery compartment of the *R-7*, representative of how the compartment would have been set up for a meal. 44

Figure 29. The engine room of the *R-14*, looking aft. 45

Figure 30. A view of the captain's bunk in the forward battery compartment. 54

Figure 31. Seaman 1c Raymond R. Suess standing near the *R-14*'s 3"/50 caliber deck gun. 55

Figure 32. A view of the radio room, not much larger than a phone booth, in the aft port corner of the control room. 58

Figure 33. The print of the sailing photo from the Suess Family Collection in the possession of Ric Hedman. 63

Figure 34. A closeup of the sailing photo, showing Lieutenant. Douglas (without hat) and an unidentified sailor on the bridge. 64

Figure 35. Jim Christley's illustration of the sailing rig.. 64

Figure 36. Photo looking aft from the main deck of *R-14* during the return to Pearl Harbor, 15-17 May 1921.. 67

Figure 37. Crew photo, most likely taken during the return trip from Hilo to Pearl Harbor. 68

Figure 38. Photo taken most likely during the return trip from Hilo to Pearl Harbor. 69

Figure 39. A sailor working on the extended port bow plane of the *R-14* while underway, probably within the confines of Pearl Harbor, circa 1921. 75

Figure 40. Page 2 from a qualification notebook of a former *R-14* crewmember. 76
Figure 41. *R-14* Fuel Oil Compensation System, Forward. 77
Figure 42. *R-14* Fuel Oil Compensation System, Aft. 77
Figure 43. Page 1 of the *R-14* log for 01 May 1921. 78
Figure 44. Page 1 of the log of the *R-14* for 02 May 1921. 79
Figure 45. The last photo taken of the entire crew of the USS *Conestoga* (AT-54). 104
Figure 46. An artist's rendition of the last moments of the *Conestoga* and her crew. 105
Figure 47. Stern view of the shipwreck of USS *Conestoga* (AT-54) in the Greater Farallones National Marine Sanctuary..106

TABLES

Table 1. Food loaded on R-19. 20

Foreword

Submarines, by their nature, are extreme engineering. At their heart they need propulsion. Massive diesel engines and their associated machinery are crammed into small steel hulls. This takes up around half of the space inside. Batteries, required for underwater propulsion, take up another chunk. And the fuel tanks yet more. All this valuable space given over just to propelling the submarine along. But what if it fails?

The unusual tale of *R-14* verges on myth and legend. Yet it is real, as told here by David L. Johnston and Ric Hedman. It is a unique story, and one which is entertaining, inspirational and educational.

Today submarine crews are drilled in safety. What to do in the event of fire, flooding, medical emergencies, gas and so much more is committed to memory. What to do if you run out of power in the middle of the ocean, with no communications, and only a few days of provisions, is not something you think of.

In 1921, the submarine was called upon to render assistance to a ship in distress. A tug boat had gone missing. Yet *R-14* would herself soon become the one which needed rescuing. Finding herself without power, she drifted, dangerously low on food and and hope. The ingenuity of the crew saved her, and their lives.

The brave tale of how they improvised to overcome a seemingly impossible situation is valuable for leaders in any domain. How a seemingly mundane task quickly turned deadly. And how a strong understanding of the basics allowed the crew to be saved.

The tug boat was not so lucky.

Today perhaps the scenario could not play out the same. The distances involved feel short by modern standards. Especially with aircraft and faster submarines. But the ocean is vast, and the same human qualities of resourcefulness, resolve and teamwork remain every bit as important. The story of *R-14* is as much a human tale as a submarine fact check. It is something which everyone can relate to.

H. I. Sutton
Naval analyst, "Covert Shores"

JOHNSTON & HEDMAN

PREFACE

There are stories of the sea that involve bravery, perseverance, innovation, adaptation, and strength of character. Some stories highlight the foibles and fallibility of humanity, and many contain lessons for the mariner that still resonate today.

The saga of the submarine USS *R-14* (SS-91) during a search and rescue operation off the coast of Hawaii in 1921 certainly contains all of those elements. It is a story unique in the annals of the United States Navy's Submarine Service and runs the gamut from simple human error to inspiring, out-of-the-box problem solving.

PigBoats.COM webmaster and author Ric Hedman first began this story over 10 years ago but never completed it. I have been a close friend and associate of Ric's since 2001, assisting him with historical research and photographic analysis. Ric asked me if I would like to take a crack at it, and after debating for quite some time, I decided, with Ric's enthusiastic permission, to finish it. Much of what you see in the narrative below came directly from Ric's efforts, I simply refined and expanded on his earlier work.

The overwhelming majority of the story was lifted directly from the official *Log Book, USS R-14, Jan. 1, 1921 to Dec. 31, 1921*. We also used contemporary newspaper articles, navigational charts, atlases, personal accounts from the crewmembers and their families, and other printed material as sources. Ric and I have always emphasized accuracy in our work as historians, and everything that you will read below is as true to facts as we can possibly make it.

However, we must insert one very large caveat: the spoken dialogue between the crew was never recorded anywhere and is entirely of our own creation. All of the principals in this story have long since passed so it can't be known for sure what conversations passed between these men. In order to provide the reader with a personal connection to the story, we wanted to humanize it a bit and thus the back-and-forth dialogue. Ric and I are both Navy veterans and qualified in submarines. Ric served on both nuclear and diesel submarines in the 1960s, and I served on a diesel boat in the 1980s as part of a 21-year career that also included tours of duty on minesweepers and destroyers. We relied on the experience of these combined twenty-seven years of naval service to faithfully as possible recreate some of the conversations and scenes contained herein.

A small amount of speculation occurs in other parts of the narrative. For instance, there is a passage where a sailor is discharged from the service, and a short time later he re-enlisted. That event actually happened because it is documented in the deck log. However, the actions of the sailor and his shipmates during and between the two ceremonies is largely our informed speculation.

There are three main purposes to this work: 1) to tell a great and entertaining sea story; 2) to provide an analysis of the events to the reader so that they may understand what happened and why; and 3) to provide lessons learned to the present-day Navy in leadership, perseverance, and innovative thinking. There will be points in this story in which we must adopt a tone critical to the crew, and this is done in order to discuss the truth of the events. Ric and I have the greatest respect and admiration for Alexander D. Douglas and the crew of the *R-14*, the bond of brotherhood to our fellow submariners being quite strong. In no way is it our desire to sully the memory of anyone's family member, but in order to learn the lessons from this incident, it will be necessary to discuss the human mistakes that were made. We treat all sailors mentioned herein with the greatest respect possible, and we would like to apologize in advance to anyone who might look askance at our efforts.

Thank you for reading.

DCC(SS/SW) David L. Johnston, USN (Ret.)

ABOUT THE AUTHORS

DAVID JOHNSTON

Figure 1. DCC(SS/SW) David L. Johnston, USN (Ret.)

A native of Dexter, MI., Chief Johnston enlisted in the Navy in September 1983. Over the course of a 21-year career Chief Johnston served on the USS *Darter* (SS-576), four Mine Countermeasures ships, and the USS *Forrest Sherman* (DDG-98). He has been on the staffs of Navy Operational Support Centers in Des Moines IA, Brunswick ME, Rochester NY, Battle Creek MI, and on the staff of the Supervisor of Shipbuilding, Bath ME. He has made four overseas deployments to Japan and the western Pacific, the Persian Gulf, the Red Sea, and the Gulf of Aden. He retired from active duty in August, 2019.

His awards include the Navy Commendation Medal, Navy Achievement Medal, Navy Good Conduct Medal, Global War on Terrorism Expeditionary and Service Medals, Armed Forces Reserve Medal w/ "M" device, and a COMSUBGRU 7 Letter of Commendation. Chief Johnston is qualified in submarines and surface warfare.

During a break in service in the 1990s, he worked in the travel, security, and retail industries.

Chief Johnston is the author of the Visual Guide series of articles concerning US submarine identification and two of his articles on submarine history have been published by the Naval Submarine League in The Submarine Review. He is a team member with the Lost 52 Project as a research historian, and is an editor of the project's quarterly newsletter. Chief Johnston is the co-founder of the website PigBoats.COM and has been a contributor to the US Naval Institute's Proceedings magazine. He is a volunteer photo analyst and researcher for Navsource.org. He resides in Norfolk, Virginia with his wife Theresa.

RIC HEDMAN

Figure 2. TN(SS) Richard C. Hedman, USN

Born and raised in the state of Washington, Ric was primarily brought up in the Seattle area. After high school graduation in 1964 he enlisted in the Navy and attended boot camp and "A" school in San Diego, CA where he volunteered for duty in submarines. After attending Submarine School at Submarine Base New London in Groton CT in 1965, he was assigned to the pre-commissioning crew of the Thresher class submarine USS *Flasher* (SSN-613), under construction at General Dynamics/Electric Boat in Groton, CT. After commissioning Flasher changed homeports to Hawaii, and from there Ric deployed on numerous patrols to the northern, western and central Pacific. After slightly over four years on active duty, he transitioned to the Navy Reserve and was assigned to the Submarine Reserve Unit in Seattle, where he completed his six-year military obligation. During this period, he performed temporary duty on the diesel submarine USS *Cusk* (SS-348), shortly before her decommissioning.

His service awards include the Navy Meritorious Unit Commendation Ribbon, Navy Good Conduct Medal, National Defense Service Medal, Armed Forces Expeditionary Medal, and the Korean Defense Service Medal. He is qualified in submarines.

While in civilian life he worked in various professions, learning skills that later served him well. An avid sailor, he operated his own business performing yacht and small boat repair, and lived on and operated his own sailboat for ten years. Transitioning jobs once again, he spent 14 years in the Bio-Tech industry in the Materials Management role, taking several companies from their startup phases into Food & Drug Administration-approved production of their products.

During this time Ric developed a passion for the early history of the submarine service and began producing a small web page about that era, learning as he went along. This culminated in the creation of PigBoats.COM with author and historian David Johnston. Along the way he has collaborated with numerous authors on submarine history matters, serving as a technical advisor on approximately a dozen books and manuscripts. He is a member of the local Seattle base of the United States Submarine Veterans, Inc. and has been its Base Commander on three different occasions. He resides in Mountlake Terrace, WA.

AUTHORS' NOTES & ACKNOWLEDGEMENTS

DAVE

One lazy summer afternoon when I was eight years old, I found myself bored, so I starting perusing my father's book collection looking for something to pass the time. There I found a first edition copy of *On The Bottom*, written in 1929 by Edward Ellsberg. It was the story of the sinking and salvage of the submarine USS *S-51 (SS-162)* in 1925 and 1926. I found it utterly fascinating and I quickly read it from cover to cover. I didn't fully understand it at first, as there were some advanced technical stuff in it, but it proved to be the genesis of a life-long fascination with the sea and submarines. It lead me to join the Navy in 1983 and volunteer for submarine service. That early fascination stayed with me throughout my service and in later years. I became a devoted historian, with *On The Bottom* becoming a valued member of my library.

Ric Hedman was the original author of this work. He completed the majority of the research and wrote about thirty-two pages of narrative before experiencing a severe case of writer's block. I have been working with Ric as a partner on the web page PigBoats.COM for twenty years, and one day a few years back Ric approached me about finishing the story, which I found fascinating. Still on active duty with the Navy at the time, the project had to wait for my retirement and the completion of two other projects before I was able to give it the attention that it deserved. I took Ric's initial narrative and greatly expanded on it. Ric and I shared hundreds of phone calls and emails by the time of publication as we worked on the project, and we equally share in the content of this work, of which we are very proud.

Roy Trent Gallemore's family have been key contributors of information. The willingness of Roy's grandchildren and great grandchildren Bruce Gallemore, Roy A. Smith, and Katie Eliot to help us and provide insights into their grandfather's history and character were a key to success. We would like to pass on to them our sincere thanks and appreciation.

Noted historian Jim Christley provided background information on the technical aspects of the R-class submarines and his willing assistance is greatly appreciated. His illustrations greatly enhance our work, and for that we are very grateful. Michael Mohl, the webmaster of the submarine pages at Navsource.org, contributed photos and his pages provided very useful research. Author William Tidd took information from the logs and meticulously created the graphic in Part One that shows the *R-14*'s track. My wife Theresa Street was my editor and coach. Her help, encouragement, and guidance were of inestimable value.

Lastly, to Alexander Dean Douglas, Roy Trent Gallemore, Harry Woodworth, and the entire 1921 crew of the *R-14*, Ric and I would like to express our admiration and gratitude for the lessons in perseverance, innovative thinking, and seamanship. We hope that through this narrative you will not be forgotten.

DCC(SS/SW) David L. Johnston, USN (Ret.)—August 2021

Ric

Without the tremendous assistance of Dave Johnston, this work would never have seen the light of day. I knew when writing it I didn't have the right line of attack on the story and I had wanted it to be more than I had been able to come up with.

The story began years prior when I was just starting the web page "Through the Looking Glass", which later morphed into PigBoats.COM. In about 2000, along with my local submarine veterans' group, we made a visit to the USS *Alabama* (SSBN-731) when she visited Seattle. In the Chief's Mess, I saw a framed copy of the famous photo of the *R-14* under sail. I was fascinated with it and it proved to be an inspiration. A few years later I was contacted by Robert Suess, son of Raymond Suess, who had been aboard the *R-14* during the incident and had gotten himself immortalized as the man standing in the foreground of the sailing photo. Robert Suess had no one in his family who wanted his dad's submarine photo collection (many crew and interior images) and wanted to know if I was interested in having them. I quickly agreed. This collection included an original print of a public domain photo that resides in the National Archives. I estimated that there were approximately twenty prints of this photo made after they returned to port, with the intention of giving one to any crewmember that wanted one. One copy eventually made it to the National Archives. Suess kept his print for many years and even took steps to preserve it by encasing it in an early form of lamination. There was no doubt this was a prized family possession. It is now framed and hangs on my wall. Thus began my quest for the full story.

I worked as much of it as I could for a number of years, getting all the research that could be found from various sources. I soon reached a wall knowing there was more, but I was at a loss as to the direction that needed to be taken. I tucked it away only to repeatedly take it out and toy with it. Dave and I had talked about it over the years. Finally, a decision was reached and the research materials and notebooks were packed and the whole works shipped to Dave. He has taken the story into the direction where it needed to go, and I'm pleased to no end with the results. There is undoubtedly more to the story but after a century has passed, people and resources have about come to their end. The COVID pandemic also made further information-gathering problematic. I'm hoping that another historian will eventually come up with something we missed and shine the light on a new angle. This, for now, is about as far as we can take it.

It was tough and Dave was a steadying force. With both of us being Qualified Submariners we are trained to know and understand the boat's operations to the extent that we can operate them in total darkness. We wanted to know the "why" and found that keeping on track proved difficult at times. We hope you like the result.

Along with the acknowledgments given by Dave, I'd like to include Raymond Suess and his family, especially his son Robert, for gifting the whole set of photos to a complete stranger and making this wonderful story possible.

TN(SS) Ric Hedman, USN—August 2021

ABBREVIATIONS

BQ	Bethlehem Quincy
CO	Commanding Officer
COB	Chief of the Boat
CPO	Chief Petty Officer
EB	Electric Boat
NOAA	National Oceanic and Atmospheric Administration
OOD	Officer-of the Deck
NELSECO	New London Ship and Engine Company
NHHC	Naval History and Heritage Command
SUBDIV	Submarine Division

PUBLISHER'S NOTE

The port city of Hilo on the Big Island of Hawaii plays an important role in this story as *R-14*'s emergency destination. It plays an important role in my life, too, as I spent a month there one summer long ago visiting my mother's first cousin. For a gawky kid from the Midwest, indelible memories of tropical beauty, and the immensity of the Pacific.

As a passionate believer in the importance of the United States Navy, in a decade where the Navy may well see the first armed conflict with a peer competitor in many decades, I whole-heartedly endorse the lessons of this book: both about how catastrophic mistakes are made, and how to respond to them with resilience, innovation and grace. We're likely to need that knowledge soon, far west of Hilo.

—*Fred Zimmerman, Publisher*

PART 1

*"It is remarkable how quickly
a good and favorable wind
can sweep away
the maddening frustrations
of shore living."*
—Ernest K. Gann

MONDAY, 02 MAY 1921, 8:00 A.M.[1]

It is a beautiful day in the United States Territory of Hawaii. It is a still relatively cool 76º F, with a casual southeast breeze of five miles per hour keeping the oppressive humidity manageable at this early point in the day. Along the south shore of the isle of Oahu the breeze is creating small wavelets with glassy crests. The wind is slowly pushing some tenuous cotton puff altocumulus clouds off into the northern Pacific. With the barometer holding steady at 29.90, there are the makings of a fine day here in this Polynesian/American tropical paradise.[2]

The mouth of Pearl Harbor cuts north from the south shore, with the channel forming the trunk of an odd-shaped tree as it moves up and spreads out into seven smaller bays, known to the Navy as lochs. The large central East Loch is broken into north and south channels by the oblong-shaped Ford Island. Once the site of a sugar cane plantation, it is now the home of the Army Air Corps Luke Field and the brand-new Naval Air Station Pearl Harbor, its seaplane ramps and hangars located at the island's southeast corner. On the shallow and muddy water within the harbor, a place revered by the native Hawaiian people and known to be a birthplace for hammerhead sharks, barely a ripple disturbs the surface, A portion of the United States Navy's Pacific Fleet is present on this day.

A small but growing base was established here in 1905 as a coaling station for the Pacific Fleet ships, and steady work since then expanded the base considerably, supplanting the facilities in nearby Honolulu. The Navy Yard was established along the south channel adjacent to Ford Island and it contained a hospital, a large drydock (with three more planned), a foundry, numerous factory-style workshops and warehouses, and several repair basins and piers. The fleet itself was not yet based here, but its ships made regular port calls during fleet maneuvers. Most of the ships actually stationed at the base consisted of patrol craft, auxiliaries and yard craft, and a contingent of the Pacific Fleet's submarines.

---

[1] In May, 1921 the USN had not yet adopted the 24-hour clock. All times in the ship's log are in the 12-hour format, so we will adhere to that standard here.

[2] Astronomical and weather data was compiled from published information from the Astronomical Applications Dept., U.S. Naval Observatory, Washington, D.C., and from the *R-14* log.

The site chosen for Submarine Base Pearl Harbor is on the east side of the harbor, at the intersection of Magazine Loch and Quarry Loch. It sits on sandy land overgrown with tropical scrub brush and prickly cactus, and is just southeast and a stone's throw from a small marshy islet called Kuahua. Two finger piers protrude out into Southeast Loch from the triangular-shaped base, and a narrow-gauge rail line connecting the small base to the larger nearby Navy Yard meanders south along the shore of Quarry Loch. The base was willed into existence through the discipline and determination of its first Commanding Officer (CO), Commander Chester W. Nimitz, and through the gritty hard work of four loyal and earnest Chief Petty Officers (CPOs) on his staff, who at times resorted to less than completely honest methods to acquire the scarce materials and assistance needed to build the base in this remote paradise.[3]

Submarine Division 14, consisting of 10 R-class submarines, calls the base home. The division is headquartered on the old and inoperative cruiser USS *Chicago* (CA-14) moored nearby at a narrow pier at the opening of Magazine Loch. The R-class submarines were designed and built during the First World War as coastal patrol boats, with a mission to range out from American bases, patrolling for any potential enemy that may approach the coastline. Despite their status as coastal boats, these submarines are among the largest and most capable in use by the USN in the early 1920s. They are 186 feet long and eighteen feet wide, with a displacement of 574 tons surfaced and 685 tons submerged. Twin NELSECO 6-EB-14 diesel engines drive them at 12.5 knots surfaced, and when submerged, large storage batteries provide power to drive electric motors providing a maximum speed of 9.3 knots. There are four 21-inch torpedo tubes forward and each boat carried eight torpedoes. For surface action there is a 3"/50 caliber Mk 6 gun mounted on the forward deck. They are outfitted for three officers and twenty-seven crew and are rated for 30 days at sea.

This day is a busy one, and the finger piers are buzzing with activity. The USS *R-14* (SS-91) is moored alongside sister boat *R-11* at Pier 1. The day's Duty Officer aboard *R-14* is Lieutenant Alexander Dean Douglas, USN, a short and compact, dark-haired, lean-faced native of Oklahoma. Douglas is a competent, well-regarded, and affable officer who to family and friends is known simply as "Dean." He is officially the boat's Executive Officer, or second in command; however, for the last several months he has also been designated as the Acting Commanding

---

[3] *Nimitz*, E.B. Potter, 1976, page 132-134.

Officer. Due to a shortage of qualified officers at this remote duty station, the boat's official CO, Lieutenant Vincent A. Clarke, Jr., has been pulled away for temporary duty as the Engineering Officer for SUBDIV 14. The division's CO, Commander Nimitz, (with additional responsibilities as the CO of *Chicago* and the Sub Base) has pulled Clarke to his staff in order to ensure that all of his division's boats are getting the repairs and maintenance necessary to be fully operational. Nimitz makes the unusual choice of pulling Clarke from the *R-14* without a relief in place because of the overriding need to fill the division's gapped Engineering Officer billet. Both Nimitz and Clarke are confident that the younger Douglas can handle the boat; indeed, if necessary, Clarke is readily available to look over Douglas's shoulder, review his actions, and provide advice. When more officers become available, Nimitz retains the option of officially promoting Douglas to CO and bringing in an ensign to round out the *R-14*'s officer billets, or getting the boat a new CO if Douglas needs more time to season. So far, Douglas has been performing brilliantly.

The last bugle notes of "Carry On" fade away after morning colors and Douglas presides over the crew mustered for quarters on the pier. With the men lined up neatly by division in front of him, he waits patiently as the muster roll call is performed. All are present and accounted for, the only exception being a sailor who is still in the base hospital. Orders for the day are read and work schedules and assignments are given out. The senior enlisted man on the boat is Chief Gunner's Mate (Torpedo) Harry Woodworth of Omaha. In his job as Chief of the Boat, or COB, Woodworth is the Captain's get-it-done man. After conferring with Douglas and the other Department Heads, he is put in charge of the day's work. Once the crew has been dismissed, they turn-to and begin cleaning, repairing, painting, and taking garbage to the containers on the pier. Bedding has been brought topside and is airing over the wire lifelines.

A small ceremony is conducted on the pier at 10:00 a.m. by Douglas, to discharge Machinist Mate 1st class Hugh McNamara from his enlistment in the Navy. With most of the crew engaged in vital ship's work, the ceremony is mostly attended by his division work mates. Naval regulations require that a sailor be officially discharged at the end of his enlistment before any further career action can be taken. After Douglas reads aloud the official notice of Discharge of Enlistment, cheerful, raucous, and joking suggestions of making a run for it before the Captain or the COB tries to talk him into re-enlisting fly from his shipmates. The guys slap him on the back and ask him how it feels to be a civilian again. McNamara fully intends to re-enlist, but Navy paperwork must be filed and he takes his discharge papers, hurrying up the pier and over to the *Chicago* so that the SUBDIV 14 yeoman can file them and process the re-enlistment papers. The ceremony quickly breaks up and ten minutes later, the Auxiliaries Department that McNamara is attached to gets back to work and begins an air charge using both compressors, refilling the boat's high-pressure air banks.

Figure 3. Midshipman Alexander Dean Douglas as a cadet at the U.S. Naval Academy, 1917. Photo courtesy of usna1917.com.

Figure 4. Lieutenant Vincent A. Clarke, Jr., the *R-14*'s official Commanding Officer in May 1921. A solid and highly capable officer, Clarke was awarded a Navy Cross for his actions while commanding the submarine *L-10* during World War I. Photo from the personal collection of Ric Hedman.

Figure 5. Electrician 2c Valoris E. Field on the *R-14*'s forward deck near the deck gun. When the *R-14* got underway for the Conestoga search and rescue operation, Field was the only member of the crew that did not go with the boat. He had been recovering from an illness at the base hospital. Please note that his name has been spelled several different ways on different documents, with some showing him to be "Valorie Fields." We use the spelling on the official Navy sailing list. Photo from the Suess Family Collection via PigBoats.COM.

Figure 6. Chief Gunner's Mate (Torpedo) Harry Woodworth, USN. Woodworth was the Chief of the Boat (COB) for the *R-14*; the senior enlisted man aboard and principal enlisted advisor to Douglas. Photo from the Suess Family Collection via PigBoats.COM.

Figure 7. Gunners Mate 1c John J. Dorsey and Gunners Mate 1c Winfield E. Bridges, members of the *R-14*'s crew during the sailing incident. Bridges is engaged in one of the never-ending tasks for a sailor of the day, washing clothes. This was done in a bucket with the uniform laid out on a bench erected on the pier for scrubbing. This photo is illustrative of the many different types of clothes worn by the crews of these early submarines. The environment aboard these boats was very hard on uniforms, so the crews tended to wear whatever they could find while working on the boat, preserving the expensive uniforms for formal in-port functions. Photo from the Suess Family Collection via PigBoats.COM.

Figure 8. Naval Station and the Navy Yard Pearl Harbor, summer 1919. This view is looking northeast from the vicinity of Hospital Point. In the upper center is Kuahua Island, whose northern end would be eventually filled in to form a peninsula. To the right of Kuahua can be seen the two finger piers and single building of the budding submarine base, yet to see Nimitz's full attention. Photo from the 14th Naval District Collection, courtesy of navyhistoryhawaii.blogspot.com.

Figure 9. Submarine Base Pearl Harbor, June 1921. This clearly shows the spartan state of the base during this time. On the left is the old cruiser *Chicago*, and in the middle are the two submarine piers. An *Eagle*-class patrol boat is moored at Pier #2 with the subs. Magazine Loch is on the left with Quarry Loch on the right. A road in the background would connect the base with the towns of Aiea and Kalauao to the left, and the Navy Yard to the right. There also appears to be a narrow-gauge railroad between the road and buildings. In later years a large petroleum tank farm would be built in the background and everything on the left and right would be developed into the growing base. Photo PH146-6-21 courtesy of the Naval History and Heritage Command.

Figure 10. *R-20* and R-*12* alongside at Honolulu, circa 1920. This photo provides a good representation of the configuration of the R-class submarines. The conning tower fairwater and bridge can be seen amidships. The vertical white stripes on *R-20* and the white X on *R-12* were part of a system in place, unique to the R-boats in Hawaii, that facilitated long range visual identification of the boats while surfaced. Just forward of the fairwater is the flared-out deck for the 3"/50 caliber Mk 6 gun, which is in its stowed position pointed aft. The bow planes are folded up alongside the forward superstructure, just aft of the anchor. The tube at the bow is a towing fairlead hawsepipe. The torpedo tubes are below the waterline and not visible. Photo from the private collection of Ric Hedman via PigBoats.COM.

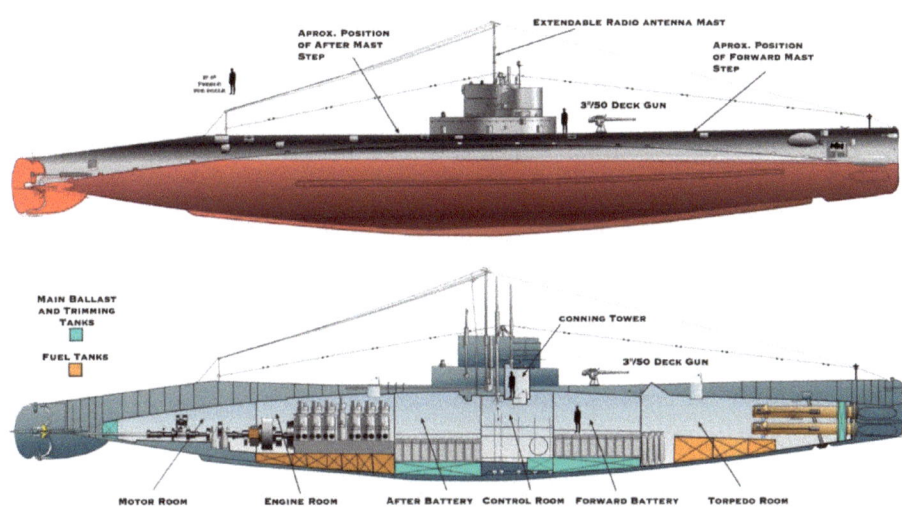

Figure 11. Illustration by Jim Christley of the Electric Boat design for the R-class submarines, as built. EB followed a very linear design philosophy, in that all but one of their submarines up to the S-class of 1917/18 were essentially scaled up versions of their very first submarine for the USN, John P. Holland's original USS *Holland* (Submarine #1*)*. The R-class successor, the S-class, were the last of those single hull designs. New USN Fleet Submarine requirements and the ever-advancing technology mandated a whole new approach after that point. All submarines by EB after the R- and S-class were built to a radically different partial double hull design and were considerably larger and more capable.

11:00 A.M. EMERGENCY ORDERS AND HURRIED PREPARATIONS

The offices of Rear Admiral William R. Shoemaker, Commandant, Fourteenth Naval District at Pearl Harbor have been alive with activity since very early that morning. Word arrives that the Navy fleet tug USS *Conestoga* (AT-54) with fifty-six men aboard and towing a coal barge is overdue for arrival and considered missing. The *Conestoga* was en route from San Francisco to American Samoa, with orders there for duty as the station ship. After confirmatory messages have been received from California, it is now clear she is at least a day overdue for a fueling stop in Pearl Harbor. Shoemaker's staff have been busy since early this morning, setting up a search and rescue plan and drafting orders for all fifteen ships assigned to the district and to others in tenant commands to get underway immediately. Word is sent to the SUBDIV 14 offices, kicking Nimitz's staff into action. At eleven o'clock preparations are complete and Nimitz issues orders to submarines under his command to prepare to get under way for a ten-day deployment to search for the missing *Conestoga*, beginning no later than sunset that same day.

The *R-11*, *R-14*, *R-18* and *R-19* are able to respond to the orders and begin readying for sea. The *R-12* is undergoing a refit at the shipyard and is unable to get underway. The remaining boats of the division are in various states of repair and unable to get underway either. Nimitz decides to go along to oversee operations, and since the *Chicago* is incapable of getting underway, he chooses as his flagship the surface patrol craft USS *Eagle No. 14* (PE-14)[4]. Nimitz and his division are assigned a plum area east of the Big Island of Hawaii, along the probable route the *Conestoga* would be taking on her approach to the islands. Confidence is high that if she is still afloat, the submarines of Division 14 will find her.

Nimitz's flagship for this operation is an odd duck. One of Henry Ford's "Eagle" patrol craft, the *Eagle No. 14* was part of a wartime emergency shipbuilding program designed to quickly get craft into the water to fight off the scourge of the German U-boats. Lacking adequate shipyard space to build large numbers of craft needed, the United States Shipping Board, acting under direct orders from President Wilson, recruited automobile magnate Henry Ford to join the board in an

---

[4] *Log Book, USS Eagle #14, Jan. 1, 1921 to Dec. 31, 1921*, page 250.

attempt to solve the problem. Ford took on the challenge and had his engineers draw up the design for a simple, easily produced ocean going patrol vessel that could be built by his auto engineers and workers in Detroit. He emphasized simplicity, so the engineers eliminated curves, keeping everything at right angles. The result was a leaky, slab-sided, boxy looking, sloped deck monstrosity with meager sea keeping qualities, but Ford was able to turn them out quickly at a plant established on the River Rouge near Detroit. The "Eagle Boats", as they were called, were actually too late to enter combat in WWI, but most served with the Navy and Coast Guard through the 1920s, some as late as 1945.

Energized now by the emergency underway orders, the crews on the division's submarines stop all routine work and immediately begin underway preparations. The finger piers become a whirlwind of activity, bluejackets and officers frantically working to meet the deadline. The air charge on the *R-14* is stopped at 11:05 and fresh water is taken on board, filling the submarine's fresh water storage tanks. The total fresh water aboard is now at 900 gallons, 200 of which has been further purified for battery water. The Quartermasters pull the charts for the assigned operation area, reviewing them and ensuring that they are corrected and up-to-date. Pre-underway checklists are pulled out and started. There is a lot to do and little time to get it done.

A major concern is fuel. The R-class boats have a normal and reserve fuel capacity of 10,383 gallons, spread out over seven fuel tanks located under the walking decks in the torpedo and engine rooms.[5] The ship's logs indicate that she has 6,978 gallons currently onboard. Normal pre-underway procedure is to sound the fuel tanks to verify that number. However, pressed by time, it is decided to accept the log numbers at face value and forgo sounding the tanks. Given that information, for a ten-day underway, it is determined that a trip to the fuel dock will be necessary to take on additional fuel.[6]

Having been in port for several weeks, there is little food on board any of the boats. Food stores ordered early that morning by the division begin arriving at the *Chicago* to be distributed to the deploying boats. Ten days at sea for four

---

[5] From a contemporary, handwritten submarine crewmember qualification notebook for the *R-14*, supplied to the authors by author Jim Christley.
[6] This is admittedly informed speculation on the author's part. There is a great deal of debate on what happened at this particular juncture, and there are several scenarios to explain it. See Part 2 for further information.

submarines plus the *Eagle No. 14* means a lot of food needs to be received and distributed. The wide variety of foodstuffs received in prodigious quantities included bread, butter, potatoes, fresh beef, bacon, eggs, apples, cabbage, oranges and bananas, in addition to over 300 pounds of ice to keep it all somewhat fresh.[7]

---

[7] *Log Book, USS Chicago and S/M Base, Jan. 1, 1921 to Dec. 31, 1921*, 02 May 1921.

Figure 12. USS *Conestoga* (AT-54). This photo was taken at Mare Island Navy Yard, California in the spring of 1921, just a few weeks before she vanished at sea. Her disappearance would remain a mystery for nine decades. NHHC photo NH71299, via Navsource.org.

Figure 13. The *USS Eagle No. 58* (PE-58), a sister boat to the *Eagle No. 14* that Chester Nimitz used as his flagship for the search operation. The Eagle boats were massed produced by Henry Ford on the River Rouge in Detroit, meant to fill a badly needed anti U-boat mission during WWI. Delays in appropriations and construction caused nearly all of the 60 Eagle boats to miss WWI, but they served during the '20s and 30s, with some seeing action in WWII. They were poor sea boats, and were leaky and slab-sided monstrosities, but they filled their intended role. Photo WT 1290-4-25 courtesy of the Naval History and Heritage Command.

12:00 NOON. PROVISIONS AND FUEL

At noon, Douglas holds another small ceremony on the pier, dictated by Navy protocol. Going against the good-natured ribbing of his shipmates, crewman McNamara, having rammed through the paperwork with the division yeoman, raises his right hand and swears the oath of enlistment, agreeing to another four years of duty in the United States Navy and aboard submarines. As soon as the short re-enlistment ceremony concludes, the maneuvering watch is stationed and lines are singled up and cast off. The *R-14* neatly backs out of her slip, bends her stern to the left, then executes a sharp right-hand turn to point herself out to the South Channel near Ford Island. She is heads out of the harbor on both shafts but running just the port engine.

She is heading to an area outside the entrance to Pearl Harbor identified as Area #6 to blow fuel tanks. This is the first part of the process to bring fuel on board. She arrives in this area at 1:00 p.m. and comes to all stop. In a procedure using high-pressure air, all fuel tanks are pressurized and emptied of the oily compensation water at the bottom of the tanks. Fuel tanks are kept full of either fuel or water to prevent their collapse under pressure when submerged and to maintain proper ballast and trim. With fuel being lighter than water, the tanks that still have fuel are blown until a sheen of diesel fuel begins to spread on the water's surface, indicating that any water in the bottom of the tanks is gone. This period between blowing the tanks and taking on fuel is the only time the tanks have air in them, because the boat will be on the surface the entire time. Once the blow is completed the tanks are vented to ambient pressure so that they may be filled. This evolution is completed by 1:31 p.m., and *R-14* is underway on the port engine alone, headed back to the base.

R-14 moors up to Pier 2 near the *Chicago* about twenty minutes later and sets up to load her food and other stores waiting for her on the pier. Although the anticipated underway time is ten days, enough food for fourteen days has been ordered as a contingency. "All hands topside to load stores," is the word passed through the boat by Chief Woodworth. The crew comes topside through deck hatches and form a line from the stack of provisions on the pier to the hatch forward of the conning tower fairwater. Men are even on the ladder and down below to handle the supplies. With the hatches being only twenty-four inches in diameter, most of the crates and boxes have to be opened topside and the items contained therein lowered or dropped one at a time down the hatch to sailors waiting below to stow them. As all sailors are wont to do, the crew grumbles and grouses as the task is performed, but privately they are very appreciative at the quantity and quality of the food they receive.

We do not have the actual list of food that the *R-14* took aboard but there is a list of food loaded by the *R-19*[8] and an assumption can be made that *R-14* took aboard a similar load of stores. It is illustrative of the variety of food they had, and to how much even a small crew of sailors can consume:

Table 1. Food loaded on R-19.

75 pounds of fresh beef
42 pounds of apples
75 pounds fresh oranges
45 pounds of bacon
2 pounds of string beans
100 pounds of wheat flour
5 pounds of baking powder
20 pounds of brown sugar
25 pounds of salt
50 pounds of coffee
144 pounds of fresh corned beef
60 pounds each of corn and peas
2 pounds each of mustard and pepper
99 pounds of fruit jam
84 pounds of tomatoes
45 pounds of salmon
20 pounds of sour pickles
10 pounds cocoa
90 pounds each of peaches and pineapples

[8] *Log Book, USS R-19, Jan. 1, 1921 to Dec. 31, 1921*, 02 May 1921.

20 pounds of oatmeal
50 pounds each of rice and lard
2 pounds of salad oil
4 pounds of catsup
30 dozen eggs
100 pounds granulated sugar
25 pounds of onions and macaroni
18 pounds of soda crackers
6 pounds of tea
300 pounds of Irish potatoes
204 pounds of butter
300 pounds of ice (no refrigeration)

R-14's cooks and stewards carefully supervise the intricate task of loading and stowing, as it has to be done carefully so that they can get to the food in the order it is going to be prepared according to the menus.

The task takes until 3:40 p.m. Bags and crates are unpacked; goods are placed in every nook and cranny. Food storage lockers are tightly packed. Finally, garbage and other unnecessary materials are taken ashore and placed in garbage bins lined at the head of the pier. The boat is swept down and made shipshape under Woodworth's watchful eye. The maneuvering watch is set again and the boat backs out, headed to the fuel dock.

The fuel dock has been a busy place all day with vessels needing to top off before heading to sea. Nimitz's flagship *Eagle No. 14* moored to the dock at 12:15 p.m. and at 12:20 the minesweeper *Seagull* (AM-30) moors alongside. Four more Eagle boats assigned to the Naval District are also present, and at 1:40 p.m. the *R-19* moored outboard of *Seagull*.

Twenty minutes after shoving off from Pier 2, *R-14* ties up at the fuel dock (Fig. 8). The engine room crew comes topside and brings over the heavy rubber fuel hoses, connecting them to the fueling connections inside the forward and aft superstructure. After verifying the valve lineup below, word is passed to the dock that all is ready and the final valve on the dock is opened. As the fueling proceeds, valve lineups below are changed and the oncoming fuel is directed to each tank that needs it. Based on the information in the previous day's logs, the process stops when 3318 gallons of fuel is received, the crew confident that that they now have

10,296 gallons of fuel onboard. Recorded performance data shows that given the conditions in which the *R-14* is expected to be steaming, she will use about 840 gallons of fuel each day; 10,296 gallons should provide them at least a 19% safety margin.

Or so they think.

Figure 14. *R-14* outbound in the main channel of Pearl Harbor, early 1920's. In the background is either Waipio or Puuloa. The white diamond on the side of *R-14*'s conning tower fairwater was a local identification scheme used in Hawaii to aid in identifying the boats visually from longer ranges. Each of the R-boats displayed a different geometric shape. Photo cropped from NH 102850, courtesy of the Naval History and Heritage Command.

Figure 15. Fuel Pier, Naval Station Pearl Harbor, mid 1920s. The pier itself is the race track looking structure in the center of the picture. It started off as a state-of-the-art coaling facility, enabling a continuous stream of railroad coal cars to be brought to the side of a ship. As the use of coal declined in the years following WWI, it took on an additional task of handling liquid petroleum fuel, with the tank farm visible to the right. This view is looking north. The present-day Dry Dock #4 would later be built in the small inlet just to the left of the pier. Ford Island is in the background. The bulk of the naval station and the submarine base would be out of view on the right. Portions of the foundation for the coaling structure can still be seen today. Photo from the 14th Naval District Collection, courtesy of navyhistoryhawaii.blogspot.com.

4:50 P.M. Underway For The Search

At 4:50 R-14 finishes fueling. The fueling hoses are returned to the pier, and the fuel system aboard the boat is lined up for immediate use. The maneuvering watch is set and she shoves off from the dock and stands down the channel, proudly the first unit of SUBDIV 14 to get underway for the search. At 5:20 she is followed by the R-18. The *Eagle No. 14* with Nimitz, his mess attendant, and his adjutant aboard shoves off at 5:30 with Nimitz's personal flag flapping in the breeze. R-11 and R-19 depart five minutes later, falling into the Tail-end Charlie position.

Aboard the R-14, the boat's only other assigned officer, Lieutenant Roy Trent Gallemore, is standing watch on the bridge as Officer of the Deck. Gallemore, a native of Bartow, Florida, is tall, lean, and fit with a rounded, handsome face. A pious man, he reads his Bible every night and rarely if ever uses swear words. A valued member of the Naval Academy fencing team (a sporting interest he shares with Douglas), Gallemore maintains an athletic physique but conversely has a reputation of being quite the chow hound, renowned for his ability to eat all that is in front of him, in part earning him the nickname "Beanie" at the Academy. Above all else, he has earned recognition as being an intelligent and capable officer, and he and Douglas work well together. Like Douglas, he is "multi-hatted" in his assignment to the boat. In addition to being the acting Executive Officer, he is also the Chief Engineer, the Electrical Officer, and the Commissary Officer.

The bridge is a small structure that sits on top of the conning tower fairwater, itself a free-flooding sheet metal structure that surrounds the vertical cylinder of the watertight conning tower, and it sits very nearly amidships. The conning tower itself is about the size of three phone booths jammed together, and contains a magnetic compass repeater display and a station for using #1 periscope. Around the periphery of the upper part of the conning tower are six small non-opening porthole-style deadlights that allow an occupant of the conning tower to see out. At the very top is the watertight hatch leading to the bridge itself.

The bridge is a semi-circular sheet metal structure designed to provide the bridge watch standers some level of protection from the wind and sea spray. It is sometimes referred to as a "chariot bridge" because it resembles an ancient open chariot in shape.

Prior to World War I, this was a pipe and canvas affair that took time to take apart and stow below before the sub could dive. Once the US entered the war, it was seen how unpractical this was and the USN copied contemporary British and German permanent bridge design ideas. It became the default for all later USN designs.

The bridge area is small and cramped, providing barely enough room for Gallemore and his lookouts to stand, their backs against the vertical steel tubes of the periscope shears. Directly in front of them at the forward end of the bridge is the magnetic compass binnacle with its steel compensating spheres on each side, a voice tube used for communications with watch standers below also attached to the binnacle. The bridge hatch is normally the only hatch to remain open while surfaced to facilitate the comings and goings of the bridge watch standers. It also speeds the process of vacating the bridge if the boat has to be submerged quickly.

The SUBDIV 14 vessels spread out once they left the harbor, each heading to a different sector east of the Big Island. The *R-14* is to search an area between lines drawn at 104° and 134° true from Diamond Head Light as a center. This is a pie-shaped wedge of sea fanning out to the southeast of the Big Island of Hawaii. Douglas lays out a square shaped grid pattern within this zone, with its center about 100 miles off shore. His intention is to search the square by running parallel tracks back and forth, akin to a pattern of "mowing the lawn". Once out of the Pearl Harbor channel and clear of buoy #1, a course is set of 141° true, engine speed of 320 RPM, good for maintaining a speed of eleven knots. This course takes them south of the island chain, running southeast until they round Ka Lae Point, the Big Island's south cape. At that point they turn due east until they reach the search area. The crew is relaxed and confident, glad that the maddening frustrations of the emergency underway are past and they are once again at sea where a sailor should be. The only edge to their attitude is the knowledge that the crew of the *Conestoga* could be in a bad way, so their amenable mood is tempered somewhat by the urgency of their mission. The wind is out of the southeast at a gentle two knots and an almost mirror-like sea is running. When all things were considered, it was a good day to be underway.

Shortly after clearing the harbor, the maneuvering watch is secured and the normal underway watch, section one is set. Two new lookouts come topside to the bridge, one with a much-welcomed cup of coffee for Gallemore. The officer watches with approval as the two off going lookouts pass on to their reliefs the topside navigation picture, and once complete he granted his permission for the watch to be relieved. The off going men quickly scamper below for some coffee and hot chow. Normally, Gallemore would have been relieved as well. But since there are only two qualified officers on board, he and Douglas are standing "Port and Starboard" watches, normally meaning four hours on watch and four hours off. However, for this underway they decide to do things a little differently, and the two men prearrange for Gallemore to retain the watch until midnight. This allows Douglas to get some sleep prior to watch. At 7:00 p.m. the officer's mess attendant brings a plate of hot food up to the bridge to a grateful Gallemore, as his stomach was rumbling uncomfortably.

The men coming on watch wear jackets to keep them warm against the coming night chill. In the tropics there is little or no twilight, and the increased wind speed of four to six knots after night fall, along with the added perceived eleven knots of wind created by the boat's forward momentum, made for fifteen knots of wind chill. It will be an uncomfortable night if you come topside unprepared.

The evening grows rapidly shorter as the sun plunges into the sea behind the submarine. The sun finally sets and the notoriously short tropical twilight is gone by 7:30. The growing night is starry with only a light cover of altocumulus clouds. Darkness is almost complete. The Milky Way comes into focus in the darkening sky as a glittering path across the black night. The waning crescent moon, barely visible during the day, has gone down while the *R-14* was still loading provisions. In the northern sky the huge W of Cassiopeia's throne lays on its side. Low in the northwest touching the horizon, the Andromeda galaxy, a pale fuzzy dot, is at the edge of visibility as it dives into the sea. Low to the west Orion still fights his eternal battle with Taurus. Bright Spica glitters diamond-like as she rises in the east and above her, mammoth Arcturus shows a ruddy gold high ahead in the eastern sky. These heavenly wonders all make a faint, ghostly light on the smooth seas. The light in the compass binnacle casts a faint red glow on Gallemore's face as he verifies that the helmsman is holding the assigned course. The water hisses as it passes the hull, the ghostly green glow sparkles in the wake as the steady heavy throb of the NELSECO diesels pushes the submarine southeast into the night, the perpetual signature cloud of white exhaust only faintly visible in the darkness.

At 11:30 p.m., exactly to Navy standards and tradition, Lieutenant Douglas comes up to the bridge and begins the process of letting his eyes adjust to the darkness, and to receive the watch turnover from Gallemore. Douglas receives status reports on all equipment, gets updates on the boat's course, speed, and current position, and chats with the lookouts as to the status of all contacts, which in this case there are none. The horizon is clear. Precisely at 11:45 Douglas turned to Gallemore, and formally states, "I relieve you, sir."

"I stand relieved," Gallemore replies. "Permission to go below?"

"Granted." Douglas feels a sense of satisfaction with Gallemore's performance today because he made the best of that pre-underway mess. He gives Gallemore a quick nod in acknowledgment and Gallemore smiles briefly at the unspoken compliment. He then scuttles down the hatch, the vision of a quick snack and a warm bunk dancing in his head.

Figure 16. Ensign Roy Trent Gallemore early in his career, on the forecastle of the USS *Des Moines* (Cruiser #15), circa 1919. Photo courtesy of Katie Gallemore Eliot.

Figure 17. The bridge of the *R-14,* circa 1921. The partially raised #1 periscope can be seen in the foreground, with the magnetic compass binnacle forward of that. On the left is the head of one of the bridge watch standers, covered by a foul-weather cap. The bridge was small and cramped and provided little protection from the weather. Photo from the Suess Family Collection, via PigBoats.COM.

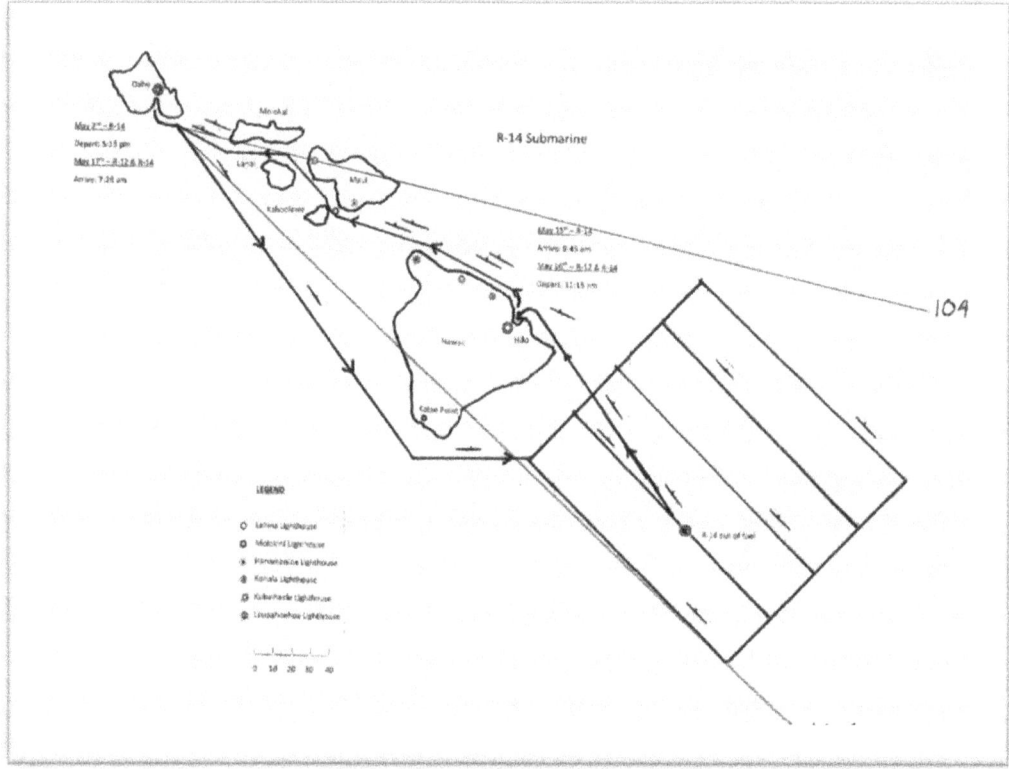

Figure 18. The voyage of the *R-14*, 02-17 May 1921. This drawing was prepared for Pig-Boats.COM by author William Tidd, using information pulled directly from the boat's deck logs. Had the boat not run out of fuel, she would have most likely returned to Pearl Harbor along the same route she took to the search area.

Figure 19. The forward battery compartment of the *R-16*, representative of the *R-14*. The view is looking aft and to starboard. Below the deck is one-half of the boat's massive storage battery, with the above deck portion being berthing for the crew. Clothes storage lockers can be seen here along with the watertight door leading into the control room. The black curtain covered the boat's gyrocompass. Photo courtesy of the Vallejo Naval & Historical Museum via Darryl Baker and PigBoats.COM.

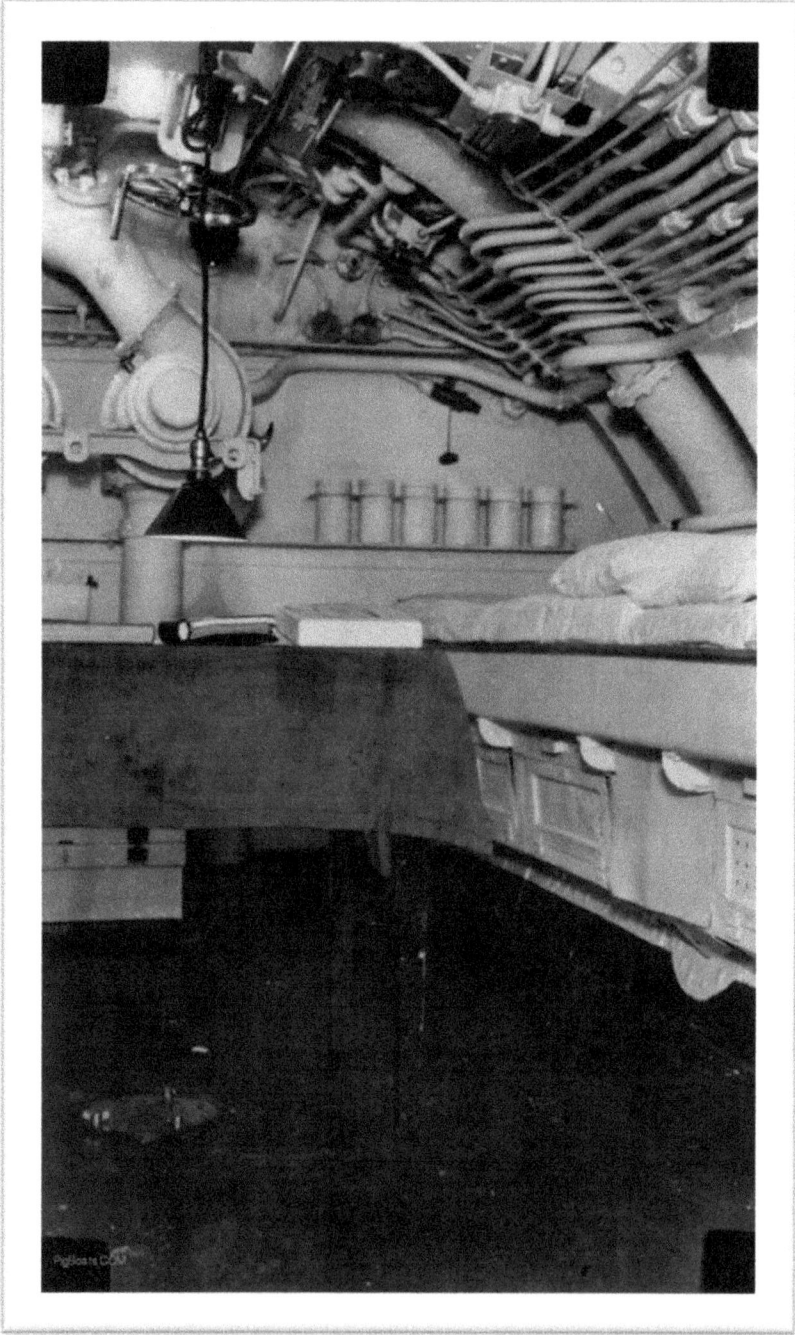

Figure 20. The forward battery compartment of *R-16*, looking aft and to port. This shows the berths for the officers on the right. Against the aft bulkhead can be seen battery ventilation blowers. A small worktable is in the foreground. Photo courtesy of the Vallejo Naval & Historical Museum via Darryl Baker and PigBoats.COM.

THE NEXT NINE DAYS

Douglas quickly settles into the bridge routine. He and his lookouts continuously scan the horizon for contacts as they listen to the melodic thrum of the powerful diesels. At 2:25 a.m. Douglas orders a 100-ampere float battery charge, a procedure to keep the batteries fully topped off and ready to go in case they need to submerge. Below in the after battery compartment, the electrician on watch makes the shift in the switches that turns the electric motors into generators and connects them to the battery circuits. He watches the volt meter and adjusts the current flow.

Below decks, the rest of the crew not on watch settles into normal at-sea routine. Many of those not on watch are sleeping in their bunks in the forward battery compartment and the torpedo room. Senior men are assigned to a three-high, stacked metal frame bunk, while the junior men sling Navy-issue hammocks from the overhead. Shoes are tucked into corners of the bunks and standard Navy-issue white cotton sheets are casually draped across the men. Because it is the tropics, the inside of the riveted hull is damp and the few fans that move air are blowing stale air around.

Those not sleeping or on watch are doing what sailors do at sea, drinking coffee from the bottomless coffeepot and telling barely believable sea stories, trying to out-do each other's tale with one equally outlandish. Some read books or magazines or play acey-deucy. Others, mostly new men, trace systems and follow pipes, taking voluminous notes. These "Nubs" or "Non-quals" are trying to complete a process that earns them the designation Qualified in Submarine Torpedo Boat Work, with the highly-prized entry made into their service records. This status is valued not only because of the extra money that the designation holds, but because it brings them into the brotherhood of submariners, an elite status within the Navy. They sit pretty much anywhere they can find a surface to hold them, or on the decks and lockers, their voices hushed in respect of sleeping shipmates.

Since the submarine is on the surface only three men need to be on watch in the control room. One is the quartermaster, Douglas'ss principal navigation assistant; another the duty electrician, who divided his time between the motor controllers and power rheostats in the control room and the massive switchboards in the next compartment aft, and the third, the helmsman at the main helm wheel. The room is darkened, with red lights glowing to add an eerie look, the darkened space assisting in setting the night vision of those about to go up to the bridge

The compartment just aft of the control room is called the after battery. One-half of the boat's huge storage battery is under the deck. (The other half was under the deck in the compartment forward of the control room, under the crew's and officer's berthing spaces.) This space is also where the ship's galley is located, along with the portable tables and benches where the crew eat. The night baker is busy in the galley baking up sticky buns, biscuits, pies, and other goodies for the next day's consumption. A non-rated seaman assisting the cooks sits at one of the tables in the crew's mess and peels potatoes, getting them ready for cooking on the boat's large electric range. They will be fried with butter on the range's grill making home fries to go with eggs, bacon and maybe some of the infamous bully beef, known by many as corned beef. Four meals are served each day: breakfast, lunch, dinner, and midnight rations, also known as "mid-rats" or "soup-down". Soup, bread, cold cuts, and hard-boiled eggs are made available to the crews going on and coming off watch at midnight. A huge urn of hot coffee is available twenty-four hours a day.

There is little compensation that can be offered to the crew of a submarine to make up for small, cramped, damp spaces, and good food is one way of doing this. Yet in 1921 there still isn't an effective means of keeping fresh food and meats aboard for long periods. Refrigeration plants are a very new technology and too large for these small subs so iceboxes were used and not always effectively or successfully. Food spoilage is a constant concern. The *R-14* received an allotment of several hundred pounds of the ice prior to getting underway and this has served to mitigate spoilage somewhat.

03 May 1921 dawns on a glassy sea with long, low swells and a stippling of clouds that cover about 40 percent of the sky, white against an otherwise blue Hawaiian sky. Once the boat arrives in the search square, they begin the laborious process of sweeping the sea, on the lookout for any signs of the missing *Conestoga* and her fifty-six crewmen. Back and forth they "mow the lawn" in the search area;

the Officer of the Deck and the lookouts constantly straining to pick up even the slightest hint of their missing shipmates. The men turn down the brims of their white hats to afford some level of protection to their faces and ears from the relentless sun and to give shade to the eyes squinting at the highly reflective glitter of the sea's surface. Hour after hour this goes on. Men give relief to their eyes and arms by lowering the glasses and blinking quickly; some rub their tired eyes. They then shake and flex their arms to restore circulation and relieve muscle cramps. They twist necks to try and pop out kinks, lick their lips and once more raise the glasses to look for any sign of their brother sailors alone on this huge sea.

Sometimes the boat runs on one engine, sometimes both. For several hours each night the boat comes to all stop and "lays to", or just drifts. This is done so that they will not accidentally miss the *Conestoga* in the black of night and sail right on past. As morning twilight appears, they get underway again for the active search. Battery charges are started and completed, and occasional minor repairs to equipment are conducted, with the high-pressure air compressors seeming to be a constant headache.

Ominously, there are several occasions when the engines begin to run roughly. Troubleshooting finds water in the fuel, and clearing this condition requires the boat to come to all stop and drift until the fuel lines were flushed and the condition corrected. With the sub rolling gently in the long, smooth Pacific swells the men sweat in the stiflingly hot atmosphere of the 15-foot diameter, tapering confines of the engine room. The diesels are too hot to touch after hours of continuous running, the temperature in the room soaring as high as 130° in the tropical weather. Engineman 1st Class Roy P. Emerline from New London, Connecticut has his work cut out for him and his crew of Fireman Strikers. Strikers are junior enlisted non-petty officers who want to learn one of the engineering rates such as Engineman, Machinist Mate, or Electrician's Mate. The men shut down the engines and begin tracing out all the usual suspects where dirt or water in the fuel may be affecting the flow to the diesels. There are a number of inline particulate fuel oil filters that the fuel passes through before it reaches the two gravity feed tanks located high on the forward engine room bulkhead. Those filters, however, are for removing dirt and other particulates only. Centrifugal fuel purifiers designed to separate fuel from water had not yet been incorporated into the sub's equipment. The two gravity tanks not only feed fuel directly to the engines, but also serve as a fuel/water separation point, with the lighter fuel floating on the heavier water. At regular intervals the water must be drained off the bottom of the tank. If the crew is not diligent in this task, water can be ingested into the engines, a potentially disastrous situation.

On the 6th the cooks conduct an inspection of the food storage areas and discover that twelve pounds of fresh beef, six cans of condensed milk, twelve pounds of butter, 50 pounds of potatoes, and nine pounds of jam are unfit for human consumption. They report this to the boat's Commissary Officer, Gallemore, who approves the disposal of the rotten food. It is brought topside and tossed unceremoniously into the sea.

On 08 May at 8:10 a.m. the *R-14* encounters a Matson Line passenger steamer heading southwest. They close the ship in an attempt to communicate, but semaphore signals are ignored and both ships continue on their way.

On the 8:00 p.m. to midnight watch on the 10th Gallemore makes the following entry in the log: "Laying to as before southeast of Hawaii. Blew water from Fuel Oil Tanks 4,5, & 6. Blew oil from #7 to #4&5 and flooded remaining after tanks." This is a routine process of shifting fuel from the reserve tanks to the main fuel tanks as needed. Any hints that trouble was brewing are apparently missed during this time.

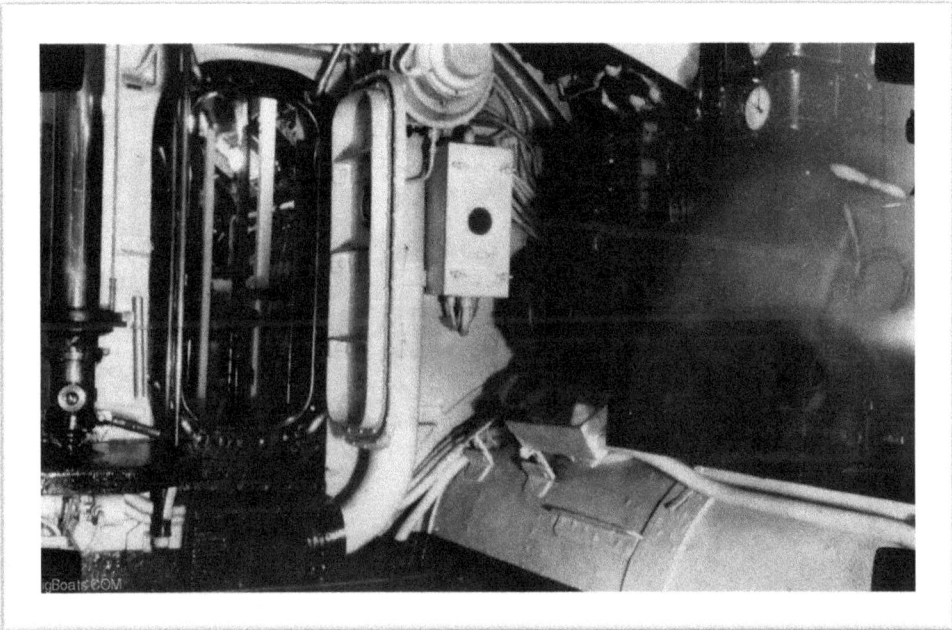

Figure 21. The after battery compartment of the *R-16,* looking forward and to starboard. The other half of the boat's main storage battery was below this deck. The upper portion contained electrical controls, the galley, food storage lockers, and the messing space. On the right in this photo is a portion of the main electrical switchboard, with open knife switches and exposed wiring. The door to the control room can be seen, with battery ventilation blowers above the door. On the far left is one of the three periscopes. This periscope was removed after a few years, its location and length rendering it ineffective. Photo courtesy of the Vallejo Naval & Historical Museum via Darryl Baker and PigBoats.COM.

Figure 22. The boat's diving control station, port side of the control room. The wheel on the right controlled the bow diving planes, which were used to adjust the boat's overall depth. The wheel on the left was for the stern planes, which controlled the boat's fore and aft angle. Two depth gauges can be seen in the center, along with plane angle indicators and a voice tube above the stern planes wheel. Photo courtesy of the Vallejo Naval & Historical Museum via Darryl Baker and PigBoats.COM.

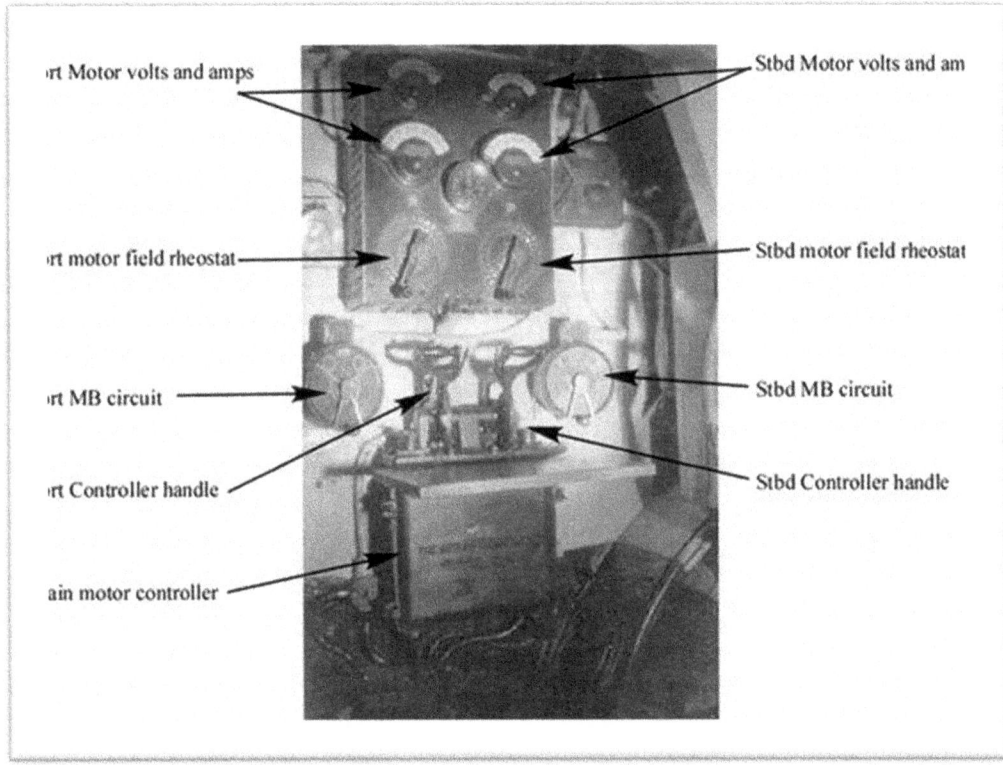

Figure 23. The boat's electrical speed controls, located on the aft bulkhead in the control room. These controls were used to regulate the electricity that flowed to the main motors that were driving the propeller shafts. Photo identification courtesy of Jim Christley, photo from the Suess Family Collection via PigBoats.COM.

Figure 24. The control room of the *R-16,* again representative of the R-class. This view is looking aft down the starboard side with the door to the after battery behind the crewman. On the right is the ladder going up to the conning tower, behind that is one of the three periscopes, partially lowered. Behind the sailor off his left hip is the radio shack. To the left of the crewman are large levers that control the Kingston valves for the ballast tanks. Photo courtesy of the Vallejo Naval & Historical Museum via Darryl Baker and PigBoats.COM.

Figure 25. Kingston valve control levers, aft starboard corner of the control room. These levers operated large, heavy valves that closed off the bottom of the main ballast tanks, keeping the tanks from flooding until the valves were opened. These levers were mechanically linked to the large valves below, and it took a tremendous amount of force and a strong crewman to operate them. Photo courtesy of the Vallejo Naval & Historical Museum via Darryl Baker and PigBoats.COM.

Figure 26. Photo taken aboard the *R-14,* showing the ballast control manifold, forward starboard corner of the control room. The controls for the regulator pump (also known as the "trim" pump) are in the large box above. This station was used to pump water between various trimming tanks forward, amidships, and aft in order to regulate the boat's buoyancy. To the left of the pump controller can be seen a signal flag locker. Photo from the Suess Family Collection via PigBoats.COM.

Figure 27. The aft port corner of the after battery compartment on *R-16,* showing the boat's galley. All of the food for the entire crew was prepared here in this tiny space. A toaster can be seen sitting on top of the range. A sink was to the right, along with food and dish storage lockers. Photo courtesy of the Vallejo Naval & Historical Museum via Darryl Baker and Pig-Boats.COM.

Figure 28. The after battery compartment of the *R-7*, representative of how the compartment would have been set up for a meal. Removeable messing tables have been set up, and a large coffee urn can be seen in the background, providing endless quantities of that most vital liquid. The door to the engine room can be seen, along with the ice box "refrigerator" door in the back corner. A cake is sitting on the workbench next to a vice. Living, eating, and working were all done in the same space. Photo from the private collection of Ric Hedman.

Figure 29. The engine room of the *R-14*, looking aft. Although a 1939 photo, the configuration was little changed from 1921. These are the NELSECO 6-EB-14 diesel engines that served the boat throughout her career. Underneath these engines were four of the boat's fuel tanks. Along with deafening noise levels and sweltering heat, the open valve rocker arms and exposed moving parts would have made a modern OSHA inspector shudder. Just behind the standing sailor is the door to the motor room. That compartment contained the main electrical motors used to propel the ship while submerged, along with air compressors and the steering gear. Photo courtesy of the Life Magazine Collection, in the public domain via Navsource.org.

JOHNSTON & HEDMAN

WEDNESDAY, 11 MAY 1921, 140 MILES SOUTHEAST OF HAWAII

The day dawns as all the others have, the short twilight preceding the powerful rays of the sun as it climbs above the eastern horizon. A light breeze of two knots is doing a poor job of relieving the heat, soon to climb to 84°. Douglas and Gallemore once again alter the watch schedule, with Gallemore having the midnight to 4:00 a.m., Douglas the 4:00 to 8:00 a.m., and Gallemore the 8:00 to noon. After a quick lunch, Douglas once again ascends the ladder up from the control room, through the conning tower, and up to the bridge. After the customary turnover of conditions, Douglas assumes the watch and Gallemore lays below to quell his growing hunger.

The search and the routine of the voyage continues this morning with no results. There is a growing anticipation of heading back to Pearl tomorrow, the initial satisfaction of being underway having been worn away by the routine and lack of results.

At 3:45 p.m. Gallemore again assumes the watch, anticipating another four boring hours of steaming around, poking holes in the Pacific Ocean. Just two hours later, his mind fighting the numbness of the routine, Gallemore suddenly stands upright as he hears the engines begin to sputter and cough and suddenly quit. A hurried and somewhat resigned report is immediately received from the engine room that they had to shut down the engines because of water in the fuel. Gallemore acknowledged the report and orders all stop. The boat drifts gently in the swells for only a short time. Just six minutes later they are underway again on both engines, the problem apparently quickly resolved.

Just twenty minutes later, at 6:10, the engine room calls up again and reports that they had to shut down the starboard engine because they were "unable to get sufficient fuel." Troubleshooting on the starboard side fuel system begins immediately as they continue on the port engine. At 7:22 the port engine sputters and dies "because of no fuel" and the boat comes to all stop, dead-in-the-water. At this point there is most likely an assumption that water is once again in the fuel system, and Douglas comes up to the bridge to relieve Gallemore, sending his

Engineering Officer below with instructions to investigate what is going on and orders him to get it straightened out ASAP.

11 May 1921, 9:15 p.m. "Hoist With Our Own Petard"[9]

A haggard and sweaty Gallemore returns to the bridge a little over an hour later, wiping his moist brow with a dirty rag. He gives Douglas a worried roll of his eyes and then looks downward. Picking up on the cue, Douglas turns to the lookouts and says, "Lay below to the control room. I will call in a few minutes to have you come back up."

With a quick "Aye, aye," both lookouts scuttle down the ladder. A few seconds later, assured of privacy, Douglas speaks to Gallemore, trying desperately to tamp down his growing concern. "All right, Roy. What the hell is going on?"

"Well sir, we are just plain out of fuel. Chief Graham, along with Emerline and McNamara, went and sounded all of the tanks using the sounding manifolds. I looked over their shoulders and verified what they were seeing. Nothing but water. The reserve tanks #1 and #7 should have approximately 1000 gallons in them, but they are full of comp water."

"Didn't you blow fuel from #7 last night?'

"We thought we did. By our estimate we pretty well emptied #7 into 4 and 5, but it looks now like we blew nothing but water."

"For pity's sake, Roy! How did this happen?" Douglas's voice rising as he fought to stay calm.

"Dean…" Gallemore's head drops and he sighs heavily, "I just don't know. The only thing that makes sense is that the two reserve tanks, which we thought were already full when we fueled, were in fact filled with only compensation water and empty of fuel."

---

[9] This entire section, "Hoist with our own petard" was entirely of our own creation. No record remains of what transpired between Douglas and Gallemore during this tense period, but we believe that all of it can be safely inferred based on our research into the characters of these two men and our first-hand knowledge of the culture of the Navy.

"But how...", Douglas pauses, calming his thoughts and holding up his hand to stave off a reply from Gallemore, realizing that pursuing blame at this point is useless. He takes several deep breaths before he looks back at his dejected Engineering Officer, the responsibility of what happened obviously weighing heavily on the still young Floridian. "What is the current status of the battery?"

"Current specific gravity is 1.145 forward and 1.130 aft. Pretty much a full can, but given our current position it isn't enough to get us all the way back, even if we go to the nearest port, which is Hilo. Lighting and cooking alone will draw that down further. We won't make it on the battery."

Douglas mulls this for a moment, calculations whirring in his head. "Right. If we shut down everything except propulsion and keep the speed to three knots, we might get 50 or 60 miles. We are about 140 miles from Hilo." He pauses while he considers other options. "Well, we can call for help, but until we know for sure that we are completely out of fuel I want to avoid putting our dirty laundry on the air." He pauses again, now resolved to action. "Get back below and find us some fuel! Get whoever you need and do everything possible. Take the manhole covers off the tanks if necessary and dip it out with a spoon, but for pity's sake, find us some damn fuel!"

Gallemore sighs, crestfallen, but after a moment of reflection he stands up straight, his discipline, training, and military bearing quickly returning. "Aye, aye sir. I will see what can be done. If it's there we will find it."

As he turns to go down the hatch, Douglas stoops and puts his hand on Gallemore's shoulder, which causes the lieutenant to pause. "Look Roy," Douglas says, trying to soothe his friend's clearly wounded pride, "It's okay. I'm a little irritated, but we will figure this out. I know you will do your best." Gallemore looks up, a thankful expression on his face. "One more thing," says Douglas, "when you get below, please find Chief Woodworth and send him up along with the lookouts." Gallemore nods and heads down the ladder.

Less than a minute later the two lookouts call up from the conning tower requesting permission to come to the bridge.

"Granted," said Douglas. The lookouts are accompanied by the Chief of the Boat. "Ah, Chief Woodworth. Thanks for coming up." Douglas quickly explains what is going on and passes on further instructions. "Go below and pass the word. Kill all the lights and anything electrical. Hand lanterns only. We need to preserve the battery. Have the cooks make sandwiches and cold coffee if anyone needs to eat. Keep everyone out of the way of the engine room crew as they sound the tanks. Stomp on anyone who even looks like they are worried. Reassure them and stay positive. We are going to fix this somehow."

"No problem sir. I'll make it happen. Permission to go below?" Douglas nods and Woodworth bends his lanky frame and immediately heads below. Douglas once again looks out at the dark sea, and chuckles quietly to himself at a line from Shakespeare's *Hamlet* that commented on the irony of getting yourself into trouble.

"Hoist by our own petard," Douglas mutters softly, smiling ruefully and shaking his head. [10]

---

[10]. Let it work,
For 'tis the sport to have the engineer
Hoist with his own petard; and 't shall go hard
But I will delve one yard below their mines
And blow them at the moon.
—Shakespeare, *Hamlet*, Act III, Scene 4, line 230.

A "petard" is a bomb, and "hoist" is "to lift", so an "enginer" is an inventor, or engineer, who is blown up with his own device. Douglas's remark is quite apropros as a reflection on an engineering failure.

NIGHT OF 11-12 MAY 1921, ADRIFT

Gallemore and the engineers work through the night, checking into every fuel tank by securing the compensation water system, venting the tanks, and removing the manhole inspection covers. All seven tanks are full, but only with oily water[11]. Chief Graham estimates that even if they somehow are able to draw off what little fuel they do find, they will have to let it settle for a few days to adequately separate from the water, and even then they may get ten gallons if they are lucky. That won't even get them a few minutes of steaming. Meanwhile, Douglas decides that a message needs to be sent to SUBDIV 14 via the wireless describing their situation. Electrician's Mate 1st class (Radio) Raymond W. Waldron fires up the radio down below in the control room, but reports that due to several hard to trace floating grounds in the set, he can't verify that the message went out, and regardless he did not receive a reply.[12]

By 4:00 a.m. Douglas has been on watch on the bridge for eight hours and is tired. He know Gallemore is exhausted. He orders Gallemore to stand down and hit the rack for a nap, letting Chief Graham continue the search for oil. The two of them will be making a lot of important decisions soon, and it will do no one any good if they both pass out from exhaustion.

Gallemore assumes the watch at 7:45. Douglas goes below and has a sandwich, and tells Woodworth to gather the chiefs topside on the forward deck at 9:00. Douglas retreats to his bunk to take a quick nap and leaves word with the steward to wake him at 8:55, which is done promptly on schedule. The brief nap helped, but Douglas is still bone tired. He heads topside and finds Woodworth and a heavily fatigued Graham standing on the port side of the big deck gun, with Chief Gunner's Mate Sidney Wilde and Chief Electrician's Mate Joe Hearne on the starboard side. He looks up at the bridge and Gallemore is there, within easy earshot. This is

---

[11] The *R-14*'s log books indicate that for a period of over 14 hours the boat was "lying to, trying to obtain fuel oil." The passages in this paragraph were inferred by the authors because of these log entries. Our experience indicates that every effort would have been made to find fuel.

[12] *R-14* log, page 295. Douglas indicated that they had been trying to send a radio message for four days but without success. Although not directly indicated, this lack of success was most likely due to some sort of electrical issue, a common problem on submarines of this vintage.

really the only place where he can get all of his senior staff together as long as Gallemore is on the bridge.

Graham updates them on the search for fuel, and as expected reported that there is none. The six of them bat around ideas for a few minutes, none of which seem at all feasible. The embarrassing option of calling for a tow seems like the only option, but they are in for a long wait, with food and water rationing becoming a necessity. The discussion continues, and while it can't be definitively shown whose idea it was, at some point one of the six men ventures the idea of raising sails. Seemingly ludicrous at first, the idea gains momentum as the two Annapolis graduates, both thoroughly trained in sailing techniques at the Academy, warm to the idea.

Their enthusiasm for the outlandish idea grows. They know the boat will handle poorly, but the more they talk about it the more it seems to make sense. After ten minutes Douglas is resolved. He puts Woodworth in charge of getting anyone he needs and obtaining any materials he feels necessary. Realizing that it is darker than Hades below it is decided that it is better to work topside, despite the narrow deck. Satisfied that the issue is well in hand, Douglas lays below to get a follow-up message drafted and sent.[13]

---

[13] There is conflicting information on who actually had the idea of rigging sails. Several admittedly anecdotal sources on the internet give credit to Gallemore, yet they do not cite the source of this claim. None other than Lieutenant Commander Robert G. Douglas, USN (Ret.) made the claim in an article he wrote (see citation below) that it was his father, Alexander Douglas, that came up with the idea. Unable to confirm this either way, the authors have decided to make this salient point somewhat vague. In the end, it was Douglas's decision to approve or disapprove the effort to rig sails, and it worked magnificently.

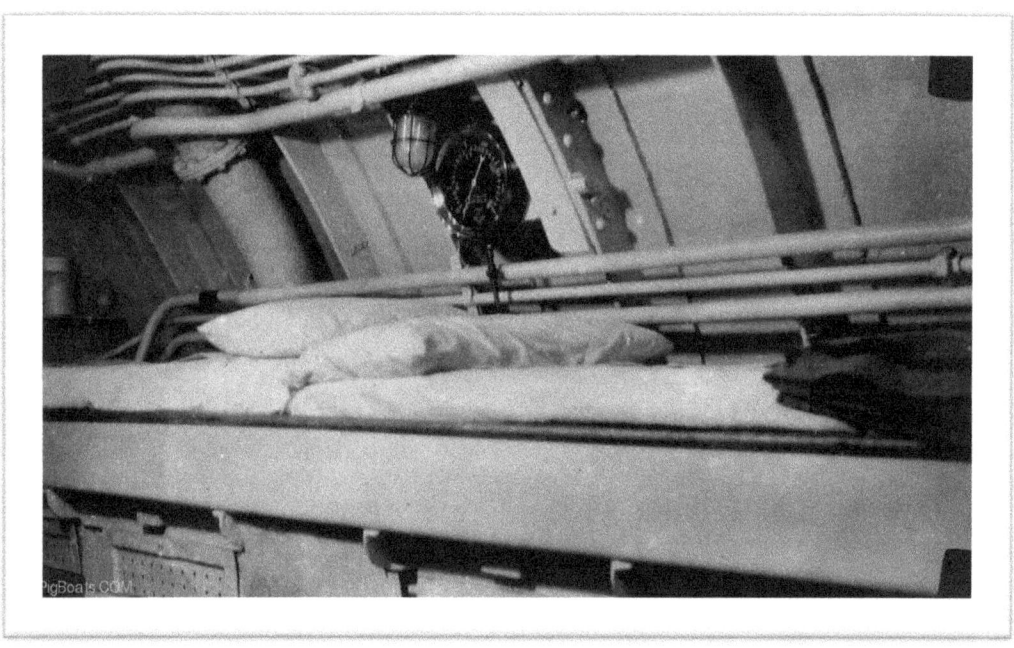

Figure 30. A view of the captain's bunk in the forward battery compartment. A depth gauge for the captain's information can be seen, along with storage lockers below. Photo courtesy of the Vallejo Naval & Historical Museum via Darryl Baker and PigBoats.COM.

Figure 31. Seaman 1c Raymond R. Suess standing near the *R-14's* 3"/50 caliber deck gun. Photo from the Suess Family Collection via PigBoats.COM.

12 May 1921, Rigging Sails

Douglas finds Waldron and the two of them head to the aft port corner of the nearly dark control room, a handheld lantern lighting the way. Working their way around the periscope and mast tubes, Douglas waits outside the tiny radio shack while Waldron enters and sits down on a small stool. Douglas holds the light as Waldron grabs the handle of an open double-arm knife switch and lifts it up, pushing it hard into the upper connectors to close the power circuit. The set hums with electricity from the batteries. Waldron begins to set up the transmitter to send the message, but just twenty seconds later there is a loud pop, a flash of blue light, and a puff of smoke. Waldron flinches, but immediately reaches back to the power switch and pulls it down. "Well, crap," he says, waving his arms to disperse the smoke. "It will take me a while to figure out what that was. Looks like we blew something in the transmitter. Sorry sir."[14]

Douglas hangs his head and sighs loudly. Unable to believe their rotten luck and knowing that they are now on their own for sure, he watches for a few moments as Waldron begins to open up the transmitter. But he soon leaves, satisfied that the situation is in good hands. He heads topside, leaving the lantern with Waldron to light up his work area. He is anxious to observe the first ever rigging of sails on a submarine.

Most naval vessels gave up sails and the associated rigging over 20 years prior, but Sailmaker's Mate was still an established enlisted rate,[15] and Woodworth desperately wishes he has one of those specialists aboard as he gathers the needed equipment. Despite the lack of traditional materials, the *R-14* still had some sailmaking tools onboard, as some of the crew use canvas hammocks and those needed periodic maintenance. In addition, the boat occasionally rigs canvas awnings while in port in order to give the crew some level of shade from the tropic

---

[14] *Submarine Under Sail,* page 3.QM1c H.D. Wilkinson, USN, date unknown. Wilkinson was an *R-14* crewman who was aboard during the sailing incident. His article was apparently written many years after the fact and contains numerous inaccuracies that don't concur with the known historical record. Somewhat apocryphal in nature, the story of the radio having a meltdown is in line with the difficulties that *R-14* had in getting messages out, so we included it here.

[15] Uniform-Reference.net, https://uniform-reference.net/insignia/usn/usn_enl_ww1.html

sun. Unfortunately, the awnings were left ashore and were not aboard this day. Woodworth has junior men dig into all the lockers below, looking for the right materials and tools, the process made more difficult by the lack of lights. Several marlinespikes and awls are brought up topside, along with two heavy-duty sewing kits that have been used previously to repair hammocks. Two sailmaker's palms are found; these leather hand straps are used to protect the hands while pushing the needles through the canvas. Several spools of leather lacing and two large rolls of marline (a two strand, left twisted, tarred jute line) are retrieved and brought up.

Down below Chief Wilde supervises the disassembly of metal bunk frames from the torpedo room, forward battery, and after battery. The canvas slings laced to the frames are sent up, along with the disassembled metal frame itself. Hammocks and the heavy wool blankets go up too.

What to use for masts? The telescoping radio mast located just aft of the periscopes is the logical choice for the main sail, and fully raised, it was a considerable height above the deck. But one sail would not be enough. Secured in storage brackets beneath the main deck inside the superstructure are two large poles. These are the kingpost and boom used to form a crane for loading torpedoes. Men open up deck hatches, unlatch the eight-foot long kingpost from its storage position and bring it forward.

At 9:30 a.m. the sewing of a foresail begins, the crew laying out twelve hammocks on the forward deck. The sail is two hammocks wide and six hammocks long, sewed together using leather laces or marline, for a total of 150 square feet. The hammocks are the preferred material, the thick canvas understood to be the strongest material aboard.

Once completed, the sail is slung from a makeshift upper yardarm made from the pipes of five bunk frames lashed end to end, with the ramrod for the 3-inch gun forming the lower yardarm. The kingpost is inserted into a socket, much like a mast step, on the starboard side of the torpedo loading hatch, and the sail along with the upper and lower yardarms are square-rigged to the kingpost. At approximately noon a breeze catches the makeshift sail and promptly fills it. With the sail set on a starboard tack a course is set to the west-northwest at 320° true. R-14, a diesel-direct drive submarine never intended to be propelled or maneuvered at sea by wind power, is now underway in a freshening breeze at an estimated one nautical mile per hour bound for Hilo Bay on the Big Island of Hawaii, 140 miles distant.

Figure 32. A view of the radio room, not much larger than a phone booth, in the aft port corner of the control room. Radio was still a new science in 1921, and the equipment was somewhat unreliable, especially in the damp, humid conditions of the submarine. Photo courtesy of the Vallejo Naval & Historical Museum via Darryl Baker and PigBoats.COM.

12-15 May 1921, Underway On Wind Power

Chief Hearne suggests a method of conducting a low-power trickle charge on the battery. By declutching both engines from the propeller shafts, the motion of the boat through the water while under sail will cause the propellers to windmill in the water, slowly turning the shafts and the connected motor/generators. With the switchboards and generators lined up for a battery charge, the rotating armatures in each generator provide enough current to maintain the batteries and make up for any power loss to lighting and cooking, as long as that use is kept to a minimum. It is a master stroke of innovative thinking and Douglas immediately approves it. The charge is started at 12:30 p.m. and as far as can be determined from the logs, it continues until just before their arrival at Hilo.[16] An exhausted Douglas, confident that Woodworth, Wilde and Gallemore have everything well in hand, lays below to his bunk and falls instantly to sleep.

A major concern at this point is steering. The R-class submarines have an electric steering system, with a large motor back aft in the motor room, driving geared ram shafts, pushing the rudder in one direction or the other. The steering motor is powered by the battery, and if energized and engaged will draw more power from the battery than can be spared, even with the trickle charge ongoing. For emergency purposes like this one, the boat's helm wheel in the control room can be directly connected to the rudder by a geared, segmented shaft that leads all the way back to the rudder ram posts. By engaging the manual system, the helmsman develops all the power necessary to move the rudder using his arm strength alone. Although assisted somewhat by gearing, this effort is akin to a major upper body workout in a gym, and thus requires the frequent, nearly hourly, relief of the helmsman.

Having verified that the foresail is holding, the crew immediately sets to work on a mainsail. This is to be made from the gray blankets. This sail is to be squarer at two blankets wide and three blankets long. The wool blankets are not quite as durable as the canvas, so using the awls and marline the holes punched along the

---

[16] The authors were initially puzzled by the entry in the log on page 287 that indicated that a battery charge was conducted. Normally the engines have to be running in order to turn the generators for a battery charge, but the boat was out of fuel. Given the circumstances, this is the only way that a charge could have been conducted. The amount of current generated would have been low and the practice somewhat dangerous due to the generation of hydrogen in the battery and the inability to vent it. Many thanks go to Jim Christley for confirming our hypothesis.

sides of each blanket are reinforced with stitching. Once again, the yardarm is rigged from lashed-together bunk frames, but this time the lower yardarm is built using the one-inch diameter curtain rods from the officer's bunk area. At 6:45 that evening, the new mainsail is hoisted to the fully extended radio mast. Estimated speed rises to 1.5 knots, still on a starboard tack bound for Hilo. Douglas relieves Gallemore at 3:45 p.m. on the bridge, and orders Woodworth and the ersatz sailmakers below for a rest, the oncoming twilight making it too risky to continue work topside. It is necessary to have a small contingent of the crew topside at all times to tend the sheets, and this watch is promptly set. What is on Douglas'ss mind at this point is not recorded, but it can be safely surmised that he feels a great deal of pride and satisfaction at his crew's magnificent can-do attitude.

The 13th dawns as all the others have with beautiful sailing weather pushing them along quite nicely, if not a bit slowly. A wave of excitement ripples through the boat when Cape Kumukahi, the Big Island's eastern most point, is sighted at 10:00 a.m., three points on the port bow. This visible indicator of their progress is vindication of their efforts, furthering their resolve. At 10:05 the sailmakers once again set to work, starting on a third sail. This is to be made from eight blankets, two wide and four long. With a yardarm made from more bunk frames, the new sail is to be hoisted on a makeshift mizzenmast made using the torpedo-loading boom, stepped on the aft deck in a socket to starboard of the engine room hatch. By 2:30 p.m. the mizzen sail is complete and it is hoisted to the wind. Speed increases to an estimated two knots, measured by tying a closed can to the end of a line, throwing the can in the water at the bow, and timing its drift aft.[17] A course change to 335° true is made.

With the electric ventilation fans shut down it is stuffy, sweltering, and oppressively humid below. Douglas allows the crew to come topside to escape the muggy conditions during the day, but safety considerations dictate that only the watch standers can be topside at night. The boat is quite a sight, with shoeless,

---

[17] *R-14 Under Way, Under Sail,* Lieutenant Commander Robert G. Douglas, USN (Ret.), *Naval History Magazine,* August, 2004, page 61. The author of this article is the son of Alexander Douglas. Additional information on how the sails were made and rigged came not only from the logs, but from a clipping from a Navy publication (the title is not indicated on the clipping), written by Journalist Chief Petty Officer E.J. Jeffrey, USN in the early 1950's, and forwarded to the authors by Bruce Gallemore, grandson of Roy Trent Gallemore. The clipping has a handwritten note at the bottom by Gallemore to his grandson.

hatless, and shirtless crewmen lounging on deck anyplace there is space. Boredom is prevalent, so they play cards, read books, and munch on the remaining unspoiled fruit in the open air, with morale remaining high despite the tenuous nature of the makeshift voyage.

For the next twenty hours, a course of 335° true is steered until 8:00 a.m. on 14 May, when course is altered to 330° true. At 9:00 a.m. the course is altered to 310° to fight a frustrating one knot current they sail into off Cape Kumukahi. Various northwesterly courses are steered through the night of 14 May, trying to beat an opposing current, and trying to keep the sails before the wind.

A half hour after the watch change at midnight, with Douglas on the bridge, there is a sudden shift in the direction of the trade winds from due east to due west within a few seconds. Anyone who has sailed a boat understands the work a shift like this causes. There was a mad scramble on the decks to move the makeshift sails from the long-standing starboard tack over to a port tack, all in the pitch dark. The job takes a half hour to accomplish. A new course of true north is set and steered as the sub sails in the dark through fog and intermittent rain squalls throughout the midwatch, the first less than perfect weather they encounter.

Still steering due north and on a port tack, the *R-14* sails on until 05:00 a.m., when the course is shifted left to steer 300°. At 5:33 on the morning of the 15th, Douglas orders ahead on the starboard shaft and holds this for four minutes, then stops it. This is done to maintain the desired course against the current and a stacking of winds. Douglas feels it is worth the risk of depleting the battery due to their proximity to Hilo, just twenty-five miles distant.

Since the night of 11-12 May, Douglas has not been able to ascertain if any of the radio messages he had been trying to send have been successful. Waldron is eventually able to jury-rig the transmitter, but they never receive replies and indeed Waldron cannot verify that anything is going out (it is not). Radio was still a hit-or-miss art, and the lack of air conditioning on the R-class and other submarines makes for damp conditions aboard; shorts and grounds in the electrical system are a common occurrence.

At 5:40 a.m. Waldron at last succeeds in getting a message through to the SUBDIV 14 Duty Officer informing him of *R-14*'s status, her previous 8:00 p.m. position (the last good navigational fix they have), and their intention to sail to Hilo.[18] The

---

[18] *R-14* log, page 295.

message is immediately given to Nimitz, who is now back in port. *R-14's* sister boat and division mate *R-12* (SS-89) had completed her repairs on the 6th and has been running local training operations since. Nimitz immediately gets word to her Commanding Officer to make immediate preparations to get underway to render assistance. *R-12*, moored outboard of the tender *Rainbow* (AS-7), immediately moves over to Pier 2 near *Chicago* and takes aboard twenty days provisions and additional fresh water. They have a verified 9944 gallons of fuel onboard, more than enough to get them to Hilo, transfer some to *R-14*, and return. At 8:45 a.m. they cast off and head out of the harbor, bound for the Big Island.[19]

---

[19] *Log Book, USS R-12, Jan. 1,1921 to Dec. 31, 1921*, page 289.

Figure 33. The print of the sailing photo from the Suess Family Collection in the possession of Ric Hedman. Seaman 1c Raymond Suess is on the right in the rolled-up dungarees and munching an apple. Lieutenant Alexander Douglas is on the bridge on the upper left, without a hat. This photo shows the mainsail lashed to the raised radio mast, with a portion of the bunk-frame yard for the mizzenmast visible behind the bridge. Without the electrically operated ventilation fans running, it would have been oppressively hot below, and the crew spent as much time topside as conditions allowed.

Figure 34. A closeup of the sailing photo, showing Lieutenant. Douglas (without hat) and an unidentified sailor on the bridge. The object in the foreground is a surface navigation light, used to help identify the boat visually at night. Photo from the Suess Family Collection via PigBoats.COM.

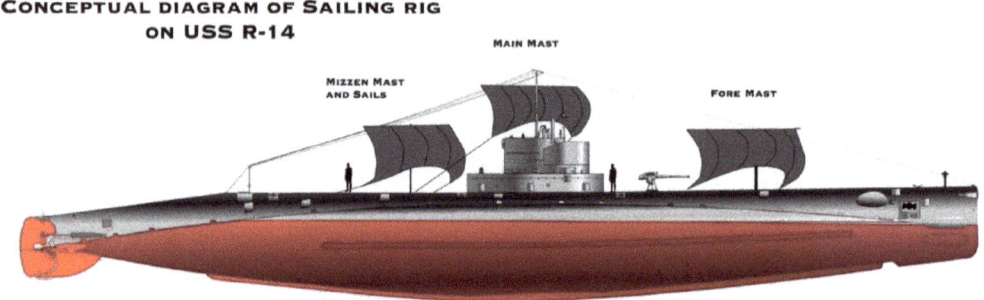

Figure 35. Jim Christley's illustration of the sailing rig. All three sails were squared rigged to their makeshift masts, and are shown here set on a starboard tack, the configuration they were in for most of the voyage under sail. The torpedo loading kingpost and boom that were used for the fore and mizzen masts were only eight feet tall, thus those sail's proximity to the deck. All three masts had a pulley block shackled to the top, through which the line used to hoist the bunk-frame yardarms was run. Sheet lines were attached to the lower corners of each sail and were tied off to cleats on deck at an angle to hold the sails and yardarms on the starboard tack. In the early morning hours of 14 May there was a mad scramble on deck to reposition the sheets and sails to a port tack, caused by a shift in the trade winds. This was a dangerous evolution on a narrow deck in the dark. It is indeed remarkable that such little sail area was able to move the boat at all, and it is a testament to the steadiness of the trade winds near Hawaii.

15-17 May 1921, Arrival At Hilo And Return To Pearl Harbor

At 6:00 a.m. Hilo is in sight on the port side. Douglas now deems them close enough to Hilo that the sails are no longer needed. He orders Chief Woodworth and his sailmakers topside and they immediately set to work de-rigging all that they had done. The makeshift sails are taken below along with the bunk frames and everything properly stowed or reassembled. The torpedo loading kingpost and boom that have served so adequately as makeshift masts are also taken down and restowed in their brackets below the main deck. As they are working, Douglas orders ahead slow on both shafts, providing a speed of three knots. Chief Hearne and his electricians immediately begin monitoring the specific gravities in both battery wells, taking readings each half hour, ensuring the discharge rate is sustainable. The course is 310° true during the approach to the long thin Hilo breakwater.

Course is changed to 290° and speed increased to four knots for the final approach to the harbor entrance. Gallemore relieves Douglas on the bridge and the maneuvering watch is stationed. At 8:20 a.m. they triumphantly sail under battery power around the end of the breakwater and into Hilo Bay. At 9:45 a.m. they come alongside the commercial Matson Line pier, throw over and double the mooring lines, and secure the maneuvering watch. Exhausted, haggard looking, and tired of bully beef and rice, the first action of the crew is to walk to the end of the pier and have a delicious meal and a beer at a Chinese restaurant.[20] Satiated, they revel in the glory of having achieved the improbable feat of raising sail on a submarine and turning a near disaster into a triumph of ingenuity and innovative thinking.

For the next twenty-two hours the boat is conspicuously quiet; just routine entries are made in the log. The exhausted crew take the time to catch up on a lot of missed sleep, having reassembled their bunks and re-slung their hammocks. Fresh water restrictions are loosened, allowing the crew to clean up and shave, and to wash dirty uniforms. The boat's arrival under these circumstances generates a lot of interest, and a reporter sends out a wire story which is picked up by

---

[20] Wilkinson, page 9. Once again, the story of going to the Chinese restaurant at the end of the Matson pier is an entertaining but somewhat unreliable tale, but we included it here for a bit of color.

newspapers as far away as Duluth, Minnesota, and Manchester, New Hampshire. The crew are minor celebrities in this laid-back tropical town.

At 7:30 a.m. on the 16th the *R-12* steams into the harbor and ties up on the other side of the pier from *R-14*. *R-12*'s arrival is a welcome event, and the crews of both boats immediately turn-to, transferring provisions and bringing over fuel hoses to transfer fuel. As soon as there is enough fuel onboard, *R-14* begins a battery charge with both engines, and this proceeds even with the fueling in progress. The electricians replenish depleted battery water, and by 10:45 a.m. the battery charge is complete. A total of 1762 gallons of fuel has been transferred.

R-12 casts off at 10:55 and heads out of the harbor, followed by *R-14* at 11:15. The boats proceed in formation along Hawaii's northern shore before cutting east into the Alalakeiki Channel between Maui and Kahoolawe. They steam into the Kalohi Channel between Molokai and Lanai before turning west-northwest toward Oahu. They are anxious to get back and their speed varies between nine and eleven knots.

At 6:50 a.m. on the 17th they are at the approaches for Pearl Harbor. They proceed smartly up the channel, and pause briefly to allow the USS *Celtic* (AF-2) to pass on her way out to sea. They maneuver into Southeast Loch and at 7:26 tie up to Pier 1 at the Submarine Base.

Douglas and his crew have performed magnificently in triumphing over adversity. They never gave up despite facing multiple problems, and their actions showed grit and determination. However, Douglas'ss tremendous satisfaction with his crew and his relief with being back at Pearl Harbor is tempered by the fact that he now has to report to Nimitz and explain how this all occurred in the first place. Douglas is determined, and will truthfully answer any awkward questions that Nimitz may have.

Figure 36. Photo looking aft from the main deck of *R-14* during the return to Pearl Harbor, 15-17 May 1921. In the background can be seen *R-12,* the boat that came to Hilo to deliver fuel and supplies to *R-14.* Photo from the Suess Family Collection, via PigBoats.COM.

Figure 37. Crew photo, most likely taken during the return trip from Hilo to Pearl Harbor. Back row left to right: Gunners Mate 2c Joseph S. Ruchas, Seaman Henry D. Wilkinson, unknown, Machinist Mate 1c Walter D. Kaessner, and Seaman James C. Russell. Front row left to right: Chief Electrician Joseph H. Hearne, Gottlieb (first name and rate unknown), Electrician 3c Percy J. Foren, and Machinist Mate 1c Dennis P. Wrenn, who eventually married into the Gallemore family. Gottlieb is not on any of the muster rolls in the possession of the authors, and was most likely only temporarily assigned to R-14. Wilkinson would serve in the Navy through the end of WWII. Submarine life in the 1920s was hot, sweaty, and dirty, and it was difficult to maintain clean and orderly uniforms. Many unofficial photos from the period show crews in this "disheveled" state. It would be a mistake to equate that appearance to unprofessionalism. Photo courtesy of Katie Gallemore Eliot via PigBoats.COM.

Figure 38. Photo taken most likely during the return trip from Hilo to Pearl Harbor. This view is from the bridge, looking aft down the starboard side. In the foreground are several unidentified crewmen, although the Suess family wrote in a callout for Raymond Suess. Chief Electrician Joseph H. Hearne is standing on the aft deck near the engine room hatch. Hearne developed the brilliant idea of charging the batteries while the props windmilled in the water with the boat under sail. Photo from the Suess Family Collection via PigBoats.COM.

PART 2

"There is so much more to learn from failure than from success."
Michael Bassey Johnson

17-31 MAY 1921, SUBMARINE BASE PEARL HARBOR, T.H.

The remainder of the month of May was a quiet one for the *R-14*, most likely a welcome respite after the arduous underway. There are only routine in-port entries in her log. Some new crew members were received, and two of the crew, Wilde and Emerline, left the boat, with Emerline being discharged from the Navy. On the 24th, she got underway for torpedo practice,[21] successfully firing two Bliss-Leavitt Mk 7 weapons before quickly returning to base. On the 25th they repeated the exercise, although this time the single weapon fired ran cold, failing to start upon launch.

26 May 1921 was a significant day. Douglas got the boat underway and headed down channel to the fuel pier and took onboard 9744 gallons of fuel. With only 262 gallons of fuel remaining from the amount transferred to them by the *R-12* at Hilo, the boat now had slightly over 10,000 gallons onboard. It can be safely surmised that an extra amount of attention was paid to this process, given their earlier experience. At 12:46 they got underway and returned to the sub base, mooring at Pier #1. At 3:00 p.m., quarters for the crew were held for a change of command ceremony. Lieutenant Clarke was officially relieved of command of the *R-14* by Lieutenant Clifford H. Roper, who had been cross-decked over from command of the *R-13*. As had been previously stated, Clarke had already been unofficially working for several months on Nimitz's staff, and the official orders now formalized the arrangement. The assignment of Roper to command the *R-14* would have been considered a lateral career move, neither a higher nor lesser command, and the authors believe this to be a significant part of the tale as a whole, which will be explained later. Douglas and Gallemore stayed aboard the boat and simply reverted to their previous duties as Executive Officer and Engineering Officer.

---

[21] The logs mention the boat going to the "torpedo range" but do not specify where that range was. The boat was underway for only 30 minutes before arriving at the range, where she came to all stop, trimmed down, and fired two torpedoes. When completed she was underway for only 12 minutes before tying up to Pier #1 at the sub base. This indicates that the torpedo range was within the harbor itself, possibly in East Loch or Middle Loch.

Roper wasted no time in getting to know his new boat and got his new command underway for torpedo firing practice three of the next six days.

The month of May was closed out by Lieutenant Gallemore with the simple entry, "Boat secure, Inspected by the duty officer."

Figure 39. A sailor working on the extended port bow plane of the *R-14* while underway, probably within the confines of Pearl Harbor, circa 1921. The standards of safety were obviously considerably different in 1921, as the sailor is not wearing a life jacket or a safety harness. If he had fallen into the water it is likely he would have been sucked into the propellers and killed as the boat passed. Photo from the Suess Family Collection, via PigBoats.COM.

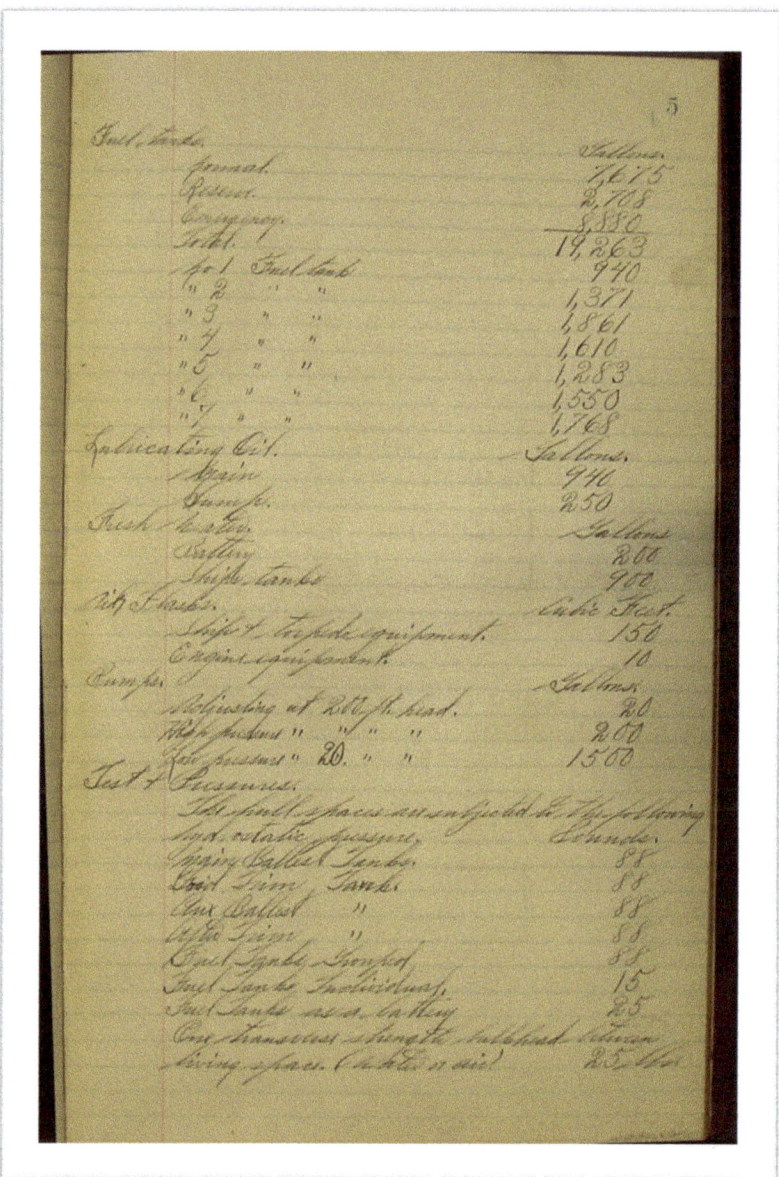

Figure 40. Page 2 from a qualification notebook of a former *R-14* crewmember. This page gives tank capacities, with the fuel tanks listed at the top. The first two entries are the total normal and reserve capacities, and the third the total emergency amount. Below that are the individual tank capacities. The emergency amount was a contingency capability and not normally used. It was intended to provide the relatively small R-boats with the bunkerage needed to cross the Atlantic under their own power, a lesson learned from the deployment of the E, K and L-class submarines to Ireland and the Azores during World War I. This and the following two reproductions of the original notebook were supplied to the authors by historian and author Jim Christley.

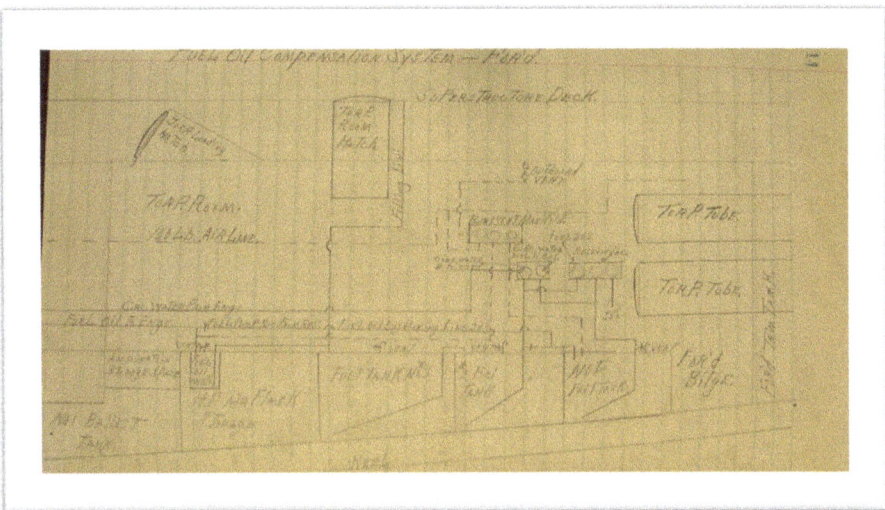

Figure 41. R-14 Fuel Oil Compensation System, Forward. This diagram is of the Torpedo Room from the starboard side looking to port. For reference the torpedo loading hatch and the access hatch are shown at the top, with the two of four torpedo tubes at the right. The tanks are at the bottom. From the qualification notebook supplied by Jim Christley.

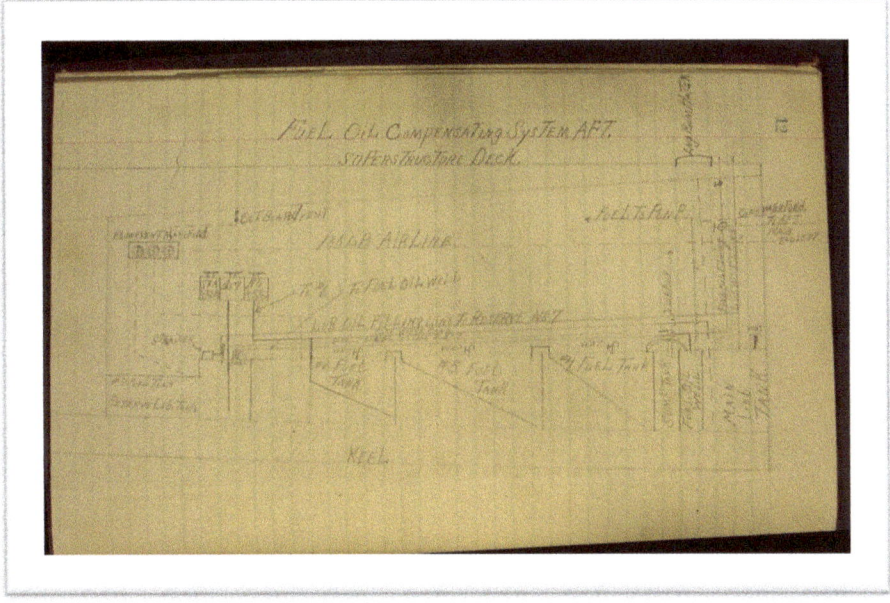

Figure 42. R-14 Fuel Oil Compensation System, Aft. This view is of a similar orientation as the one above, but shows the engine room. The boat's two NELSECO diesels would have been mounted above the tanks. Number 7 tank, one of the two critical reserve tanks, is located all the way to the left (aft), with a portion of it partitioned off as the reserve lube oil tank. From the qualification notebook supplied by Jim Christley.

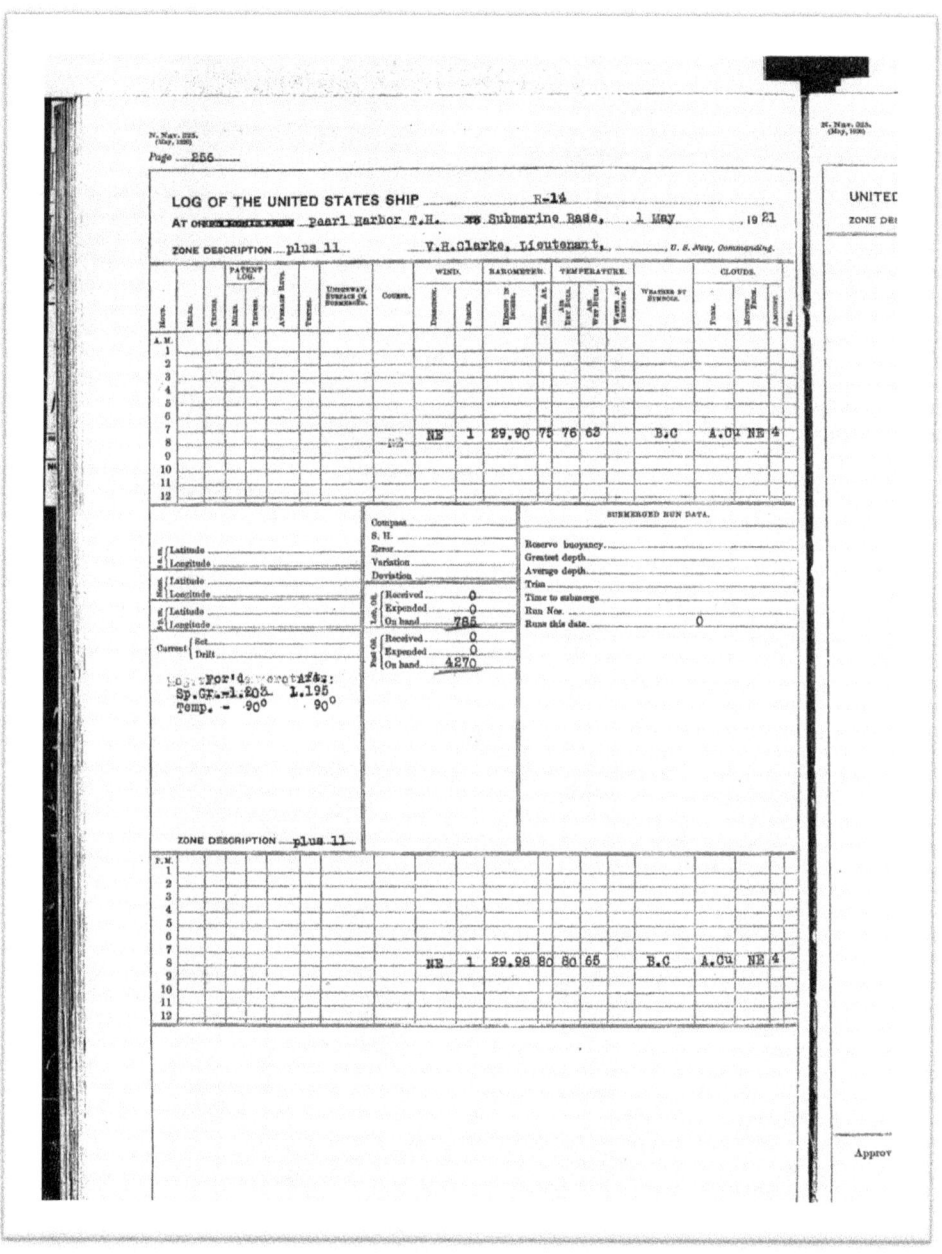

Figure 43. Page 1 of the R-14 log for 01 May 1921. In the center are the recorded amounts of lube oil and fuel oil onboard on that day. The under-strikes in this case are by the authors. For fuel, we believe this is a corrected amount, showing the actual amount of fuel onboard that day, being corrected from what had been recorded by hand in the day-to-day hand-written logs, which are not retained. Note Clarke's name, listed at the top as the Commanding Officer. Whoever typed this page used "H" as his middle initial, when it should have been "A". From a reproduction of the original log, supplied by the National Archives.

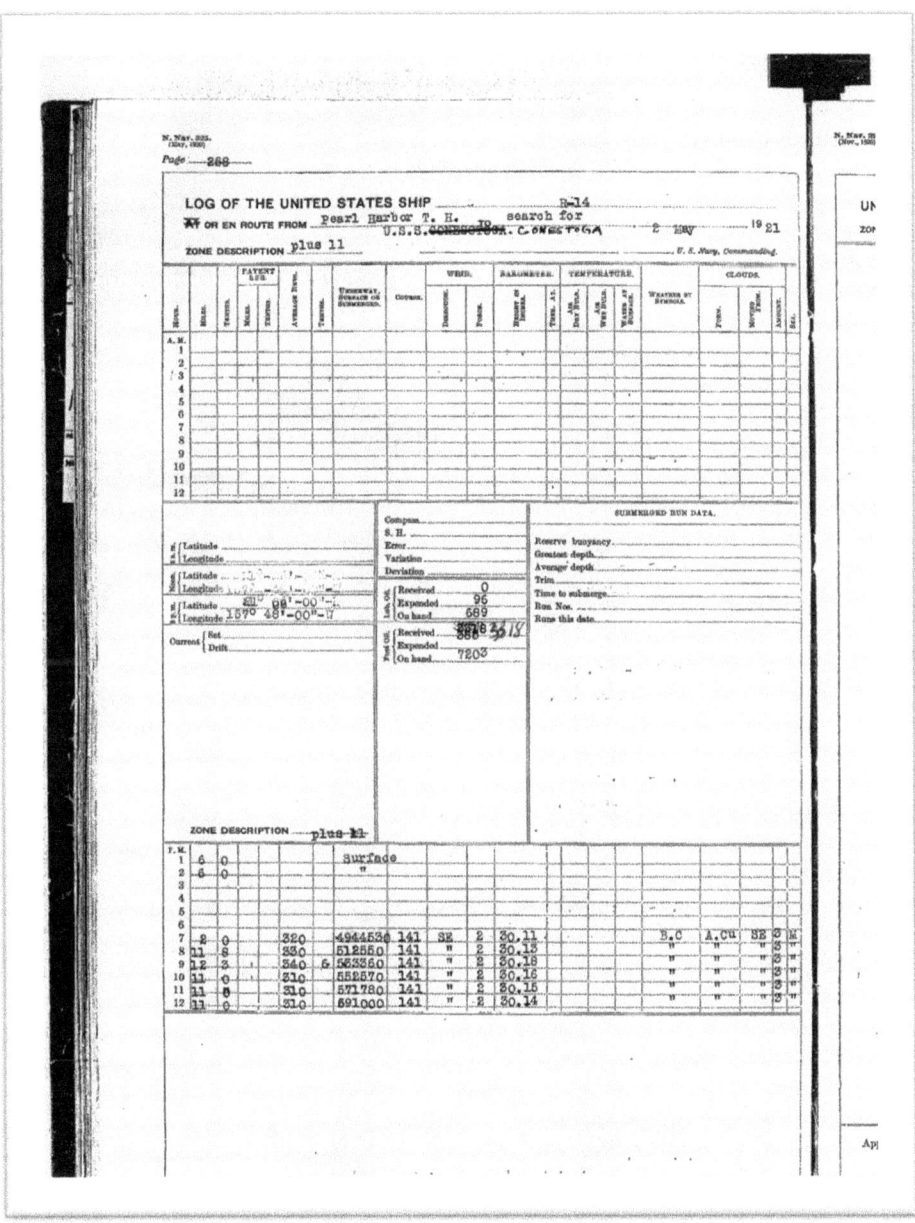

Figure 44. Page 1 of the log of the R-14 for 02 May 1921. In the center can be seen the received and expended amounts, and the total remaining at the end of the first day of the underway period. The typing overstrike is an original, and indicative of the sloppy nature of the log preparation. The hand-written note is by the authors, determined after examining the overstrike with a magnifying glass. The correction at the top is by the authors. From a reproduction of the original log, supplied by the National Archives.

How And Why

Running out of fuel at sea is an extremely rare occurrence in the Navy. In fact, neither author is aware of any other circumstances in which this has actually happened to a major warship, although given the nearly 175-year history of operating powered vessels in the Navy, it is at least possible. Multiple personnel onboard ship look at and keep track of fuel quantity and usage, from the senior Petty Officers and Chiefs in the Engineering Department, through the Engineering Officer, and all the way to the Commanding Officer. For all these men to miss what should have been obvious would be rare indeed. The crew of the *R-14* were clearly surprised at the fact that they ran out of fuel, as the logs indicate that they spent 14 hours searching the tanks for any useful amount. In addition, wire service reporters that interviewed the crew upon arrival in Hilo reported that the crew could not account for how they ran dry.[22] If the crew was surprised by running out of fuel, then the only way to explain it was that either there was a previously unknown leak in one or more of the tanks, or that they believed they had more fuel onboard then they actually had when they went to the fuel pier in Pearl Harbor.

The Electric Boat design R-class submarines had a normal and reserve fuel capacity of 10,383 gallons. This fuel was contained in seven tanks, three flat-topped tanks located underneath the torpedo room, the tops of which formed the walking deck, and four similar tanks underneath the engine room. Tanks 1 and 7 were designated as reserve tanks, with tanks 2,3,4,5, and 6 as the ready service tanks.[23] There was also a capacity of 8,880 gallons that could be carried in addition to the normal and reserve amounts, but this amount had to be carried in the ballast tanks, rendering the boat incapable of submerging until it was used up and the tanks cleared; the concept of the fuel ballast tank had not yet been implemented in the USN. This "emergency" capacity was intended for very long surface transits, like crossing the Atlantic, and was not routinely used by any R-boat. It definitely was not part of the *R-14*'s fuel loadout for this voyage.

---

[22] From two identical articles, one in the *Duluth Evening Herald*, May 17, 1921 and another in the *Manchester Democrat*, July 13, 1921.

[23] These diagrams were supplied to the authors from naval historian and author Jim Christley, who obtained them from a former crewmember.

The *R-14*'s logs provide an initially confusing picture of the fuel issue. On 01 May the logs indicate that she had 4,270 gallons of fuel on board. As indicated in Part One, after receiving the orders to get underway and search for the *Conestoga*, the *R-14* went to the fuel pier and took on 3,318 gallons, for a total prior to getting underway of 7,588 gallons. On the first day of steaming while headed for the operation area they burned 385 gallons, so at the end of the day on 02 May, they had 7,203 gallons remaining.

The authors went through each day's logs and computed the average underway fuel usage as being 840 gallons per day. This average figure would have been a well-known data point onboard. The *R-14* had been in commission for over 18 months and Clarke had been her only CO during this time. He would have been very familiar with how much fuel the boat burned during an average day's steaming. The long voyage from California to Hawaii in 1920 provided the numerous data points needed to compute this figure. This knowledge would have naturally been passed on to Douglas and Gallemore. In addition, the technically savvy chiefs and senior petty officers in the Engineering Department would have been very aware of this figure as well.

So, with 7,588 gallons on board when they got underway, and with an average usage of 840 gallons a day, it should have been blindingly apparent to anyone that the boat was headed to sea *without enough fuel onboard to complete a 10-day mission.*

The capacity of reserve tanks 1 and 7 are a total of 2,708 gallons. If added to the 4,270 gallons that was recorded to be onboard on 01 May that comes to 6,978 gallons. This is the amount of fuel that Douglas must have believed he had once they arrived at the fuel pier. This dictates the 3,318 gallons that was taken onboard at that time. Douglas and his crew thought they were getting underway with 10,296 gallons, enough for a 10-day mission with an approximate 19% reserve. It is apparent now that both of the reserve tanks were empty of fuel and full only of compensation water, when the crew, including Douglas, thought otherwise. This would explain their puzzlement at finding themselves at sea and out of fuel.

How was this extremely important data point missed? So much time has passed, and so much contemporary material has been lost that we cannot arrive at the root cause. Former NASA Space Shuttle Program Manager and Flight Director Wayne Hale once said that any accident investigation has to ask "why" at least seven times before arriving at the root cause.[24] We will not be able to adhere to that principal in this case due to the amount of time that has passed, but the principal is sound and we will apply it here to the greatest extent possible. In the case of gaps in verifiable information, the authors will use their collective experience to conduct informed and conservative speculation as to causes.

Logs

In 1921 the US Navy actually kept two logs of the minute-to-minute details of operations aboard ship. Each day the duty Quartermaster hand wrote the deck log and the senior watch member in the Engineering Department kept the engineering logs. At the end of each month these logs were gathered together, combined, reviewed, and typed up on Navy Form 325. If the ship was large enough to have an administrative department, it was handled at that level. If not, the squadron or division would handle the typing. The authors have in their possession copies of the typed logs that were formally submitted to the Department of the Navy for record-keeping purposes. Apparently, the hand-written logs were disposed of once the typewritten logs were signed and submitted since they were not filed at the National Archives.

The first thing that stands out is the incredible lack of attention to detail in the logs. There are numerous misspellings, typing overstrikes, and outright errors. For instance, on the day the *R-14* arrived in Hilo, at the top of the log page where it should have been labeled as "Log of the United States Ship *R-14*" the typist put down *R-12*. For the 4th and 5th of May the lube oil and fuel oil usage are exactly the same, with the same totals, which is clearly not possible. Gallemore and Douglas signed the logs at the end of each watch, and both Clarke and Douglas signed the log at the bottom of each page as the Commanding Officer and Navigator (even though Clarke was not aboard for the voyage). When an officer affixes his signature to a log, he is affirming that the log is accurate and true. Yet the logs clearly were not. This sloppiness in the typed logs indicate that there was not the proper emphasis on this important task from the senior command level (i.e., SUBDIV 14), nor the proper oversight from those responsible for submitting proper and accurate logs (Douglas and Clarke). It is entirely possible that this lackadaisical

---

[24] *Pilot Error is Never Root Cause,* Wayne Hale, 2015, https://waynehale.wordpress.com/2015/07/29/pilot-error-is-never-root-cause/

standard in regard to log keeping would also be found in the day-to-day handwritten logs. If so, then it is reasonable to speculate that an error in recording fuel usage or recording a fuel offload due to a maintenance period was the cause. Clearly, the crew believed they had 6,978 gallons on board when they arrived at the fuel pier, but they did not, and this is most likely to due to poor record-keeping.

Strangely, the typed logs seem to indicate the *actual* amount of fuel on board, not the *perceived* amount. For instance, on 08 May, five days before they were due to arrive back in Pearl Harbor, the typed log indicates that during the day they used 900 gallons of fuel and had 2,108 gallons remaining. With five days to go, it should have been very apparent that they weren't going to make it. The fact that the typed logs were corrected after the fact to show the actual amounts we believe was directed by Nimitz. He wanted the official log submitted to the Dept. of the Navy to be accurate in this regard.

Why the logs were in a sloppy state is hard to say. It could be due to a lack of administrative personnel and skilled typists in Hawaii at the time. Indeed, we already know that Nimitz operated with gapped billets on his staff, and even the *R-14* herself did not have an enlisted yeoman assigned. More alarmingly it may have come from a general lack of standards within the squadron or within the entire Naval District itself. This does not sound like a situation that the normally meticulous Nimitz would have tolerated, but he had only been in Hawaii for less than a year at that point, and much of his time and effort had been spent willing the submarine base into existence. He may not yet have had the time at that period to concentrate on operational and administrative issues for the squadron.

Procedural Compliance

On a submarine in those days there wasn't a traditional "gas gauge" that you simply looked at to determine how much fuel you had. For each fuel tank there was a sounding manifold, a collection of 3/8" copper tubes that ran to different levels of the tank. Each tube had a petcock style valve at the end. Starting at the tube for the lowest level of the tank, the assigned sailor would open the petcock and allow the outflow to drain into a bucket. After a set time to ensure clearing of the line of any residual amount left from the previous sounding, the sailor would observe the flow to determine whether it was water or fuel. If they got fuel from the tube representing the lowest part of the tank, they would immediately know that the tank was completely full and would close the petcock. If they got water, they would move to the next highest tube and repeat the procedure. Using the concept that fuel floats on water, they would continue this process until they got fuel or until the last tube petcock had been cycled. Which line, if any, they got fuel from told them how much fuel was in the tank.

In Part One we speculated on a scenario in which prior to heading to the fuel pier a hurried Chief Graham and Lieutenant Gallemore blindly trusted the information that was in the existing hand-written logs and no attempt was made to sound the tanks to empirically determine their levels. This error in judgment would have most likely been prompted by the rushed and hurried nature of the pre-underway preparations. The imperative to get going immediately took precedence over good engineering practice, skewing their judgment. If true, this would have been a very fateful and consequential decision indeed.

It is also completely plausible that the tanks were actually sounded, but due to the fact that more experienced personnel were working other items on the checklists, junior, inexperienced crewmen were tasked with this procedure. Not yet fully trained or fully qualified, they may have misinterpreted what they saw when looking into their bucket, thinking they saw fuel oil but in fact it was only oily water. They may also not have let the flow run long enough when they initially opened the petcock and may have seen oil left in the sounding line from the previous evolution. More experienced crewmen most likely would not have made these simple errors and would have been more diligent at the task.

At any rate, it is likely that there was a serious lapse in procedural compliance. Determining the absolute level of a fuel tank prior to taking on fuel is a time-proven and experience-honed procedure in the USN, with its origins going as far back as the coal burning days. Indeed, this procedure is a *basic necessity* in order to take on the proper and needed amount and to avoid potentially hazardous spills due to overfilling the tank. It has been accepted procedure since 12 October 1900, the day that the USN's first submarine, the USS *Holland*, was commissioned, but it clearly was not accomplished this day. Why this established and tested procedure was not followed on 02 May 1921 will be discussed below.

Blowing The Tanks

The authors considered the idea that the fuel tank blowing procedure that was conducted at 1:00 pm on 02 May, prior to going to the fuel pier, may have resulted in the crew going too far. In their hurry to get the underway preparations completed, they may have been overzealous in the procedure, resulting in not only the compensation water being blown overboard, but the fuel as well, specifically the fuel in reserve tanks #1 and 7. It is easy to see how this may have been done, because knowing when to stop by observing the oil sheen on the water topside is admittedly an exercise in judgment. However, in considering this scenario, the authors concluded that while possible, it was unlikely. Reserve tanks #1 and 7 held 2,708 gallons, and if the crew had blown these two tanks dry the sheen created topside would have been immense, giving the crew a very obvious reason to empirically determine the tank levels. The "oops factor" of the huge sheen alone would have prompted this.

Fuel Tank Leak

The idea that there may have been a leak in one or more of the fuel tanks was initially considered by the authors. All submarines built by the USN up to this time had been of all-riveted construction. The frame rings were riveted to the keel and the hull and tank plating were riveted to the frames. Welding was a new and not yet trusted science and this revolutionary construction method would not be incorporated into submarine construction for several more years. Riveted seams can, and often did, work loose due to the motion of the boat in a seaway and they required constant caulking in order to remain watertight.[25] Leakage was a fairly common occurrence. In 1941 the partially riveted fleet submarine *Narwhal* (SS-167) lost 20,000 gallons of fuel to leakage in one 30-day training cruise.[26]

However, once the fuel quantity data from the logs was considered, the authors rejected the idea that a fuel leak was solely responsible for the boat running out of fuel. The reason for our decision was the fuel quantity numbers in the logs. As

---

[25] *No More Heads or Tails: The Adoption of Welding in U.S. Navy Submarines*, David L. Johnston, *The Submarine Review*, June, 2020, page 46-48.
[26] *U.S. Subs in Action*, Robert C. Stern, 1979, page 20.

pointed out above, the crew clearly believed that they had 6,978 gallons of fuel onboard when they arrived at the fuel pier. In the course of the post-incident investigation, Nimitz without a doubt would have asked the question, "Did you sound the tanks prior to taking on fuel?" If they answered in the affirmative and could show that proper procedure had been followed, then the initial amount of fuel recorded in the official typed log on 02 May would have been the previously mentioned 6,978 gallons, *not the 4,270 gallons that was actually recorded.*

It is very important to understand that the only way that a fuel leak could have been the root cause of the incident would have been if the initial amount of fuel onboard had *actually* been 6,978 gallons, and when combined with the 3,318 gallons that they took onboard at the fuel pier, the total amount of fuel onboard when they left the fuel pier and headed to sea was 10,296 gallons. *Only under these conditions* is it reasonable to speculate that during the course of the period at sea a hole or a gapped seam in one or more tanks led to the fuel leaking out and caused the boat to run dry, *given the fact that the boat ran out of fuel on the 10th day.*

If the boat got underway with the 7,588 gallons indicated in the log (4,270 initial and 3,318 taken on at the fuel pier), *and had a fuel leak*, then the boat would have run dry at some time on the 6th day, not the 10th.

Subsequent research has shown that indeed there was a leak in one of the fuel tanks. Bruce Gallemore, Lieutenant Gallemore's grandson, provided the authors with a copy of a page from Lieutenant Gallemore's personal diary. This particular page was a hand-written recap of the events of 02-17 May 1921, and the events described therein were closely in line with the official logs. However, in the lower right-hand corner, Gallemore made a small note that read, "Later: Leak in tank found at overhaul." Location, size, and particulars of the leak were not given. In addition, during an interview with another of Gallemore's grandsons, Roy A. Smith, Smith revealed to the authors that he had conducted a taped interview of his grandfather in 1977 just prior to his death. During that interview Gallemore mentioned again that a leak had been found in a subsequent overhaul.

Given this information, it is safe to say that indeed the *R-14* suffered from some level of fuel leakage during the May 1921 incident. While a leak may have been a contributing factor, given all the information above, we believe that it was *not the root cause*. Why? Because the fuel amount recorded in the log had to come from somewhere. If Nimitz had asked, "Did you sound the fuel tanks prior to taking on fuel", and Douglas and Gallemore had answered with a sheepish and embarrassed

"No", then once again simple math would have shown that the reserve tanks that they thought were full were actually empty and this would have dictated the 4,270 gallons that was recorded in the typed log. With Clarke, Douglas, and Gallemore signing the logs verifying that they are true and accurate, and given that this was a prime data point of the investigation, we believe that these numbers can be trusted when other parts of the logs cannot.

LEADERSHIP, OVERSIGHT, AND ORGANIZATIONAL ISSUES

It has been policy within the USN since 13 October 1775 that the Commanding Officer of a vessel is ultimately responsible for *everything* that goes on aboard his ship. This is an essential tenet that establishes clear command authority and an unquestioned line of responsibility. Part of his duties is exercising the proper level of oversight so that he is informed as to the status of his command, but without micromanaging behavior that can stifle initiative and creative problem solving. It is a fine line to walk, and failing to do so in a competent manner can adversely affect command effectiveness.

As noted, there were numerous instances in which a lack of leadership and oversight occurred during the month of May, 1921, aboard the *R-14*, specifically related to running out of fuel. The senior petty officers did not properly supervise the junior personnel, the chief petty officers did not fully inculcate professionalism and the need to follow regulations and procedures, and Douglas and Gallemore did not instill and emphasize the proper command climate, a climate that promotes attention to detail and procedural compliance. Given the fact that determining absolute fuel levels is a basic necessity of effectively operating a warship, and given the fact that the boat ran out of fuel and the crew was surprised by this, it is apparent that everyone in a position of leadership aboard *R-14* fell short of properly negotiating that fine line of leadership and oversight.

At this point we must return to Wayne Hale's previously cited thesis *Pilot Error Is Never Root Cause* (sic). Hale makes the profound point that simply blaming an aircraft accident on pilot error is a vast oversimplification that can obscure the real root cause, and in doing so may lead to the same incident happening again. Pointing the finger at Douglas, and by proxy Gallemore, is perhaps only the first "why" of several more whys of this story. Those whys are mitigating factors, and once examined, will provide a more rounded picture and greatly aid in understanding the root cause, or causes. These factors are listed below in no particular order of importance:

1. **Paradise (a.k.a. "Tahiti") Syndrome.** People from Anglo/European/American cultures in this post-Edwardian period were known for their social conservativism, Judeo/Christian values, and highly disciplined ways. When exposed to the sub-tropical, idyllic "paradise" of beautiful Hawaii with its peaceful and uncomplicated environment and comparatively permissive morality, people of highly driven, goal-oriented, pressure-cooker cultures can develop a type of mental malaise. This condition expresses itself in a loss of interest in normal activities, a decline in discipline, a heightened desire to "drop-out" and relax, and oftentimes an increased potential for substance abuse. It is a particular problem within military services, and if not properly managed by the command leadership, it can lead to the very problems in attention to detail and procedural compliance noted above. Both authors have personal experience with this potentially debilitating malady while serving in places like Hawaii, the Philippines, and other tropical locales and have seen first-hand the impacts it can have on crew effectiveness. The Hawaiian Islands in 1921 were still a largely primitive and undeveloped paradise, and they had a Jimmy Buffett/Paul Gauguin-like lure to the young men who were stationed there. This was undoubtedly a factor that complicated the leadership issues faced by the officers and Chiefs of the *R-14*, and indeed by every military command in Hawaii. This "paradise syndrome" was a prime factor in the incident aboard HMS *Bounty* in 1789, and it played a role in the events of 07 December 1941.

2. **The Nature of Naval Operations in Hawaii in 1921.** Two and a half years after the end of World War I, operations for the entire United States Navy, and in particular the units stationed in Hawaii, had devolved to a stable, low-intensity and low-key peacetime standard. It was widely believed that WWI had been the "war to end all wars" and that energetic military training was no longer necessary. Budgetary cutbacks and the onset of post-war disarmament treaties had furthered that lassitude. While it was understood that our forces needed to remain ready, the War Department had trouble defining what they needed to be ready for. Routine had become paramount, with a natural and somewhat understandable

reluctance to break it.²⁷ The majority of the operations undertaken by the SUBDIV 14 boats during this period consisted of short, one or two-day training operations in the immediate vicinity of Oahu. Given this situation, it is not hard to see how an unanticipated, last-minute order to get underway for a 10-day, blue water contingency search and rescue operation could have thrown the routine of the *R-14* askew, leading to rushed decisions and lapses in judgment and procedure.

3. **Organization Aboard R-class Submarines.** The R-class submarines were billeted for three officers and twenty-seven enlisted.²⁸ However, this obscures the fact that the officers would have been "multi-hatted" during their tour aboard, filling multiple collateral duties as required by Naval Regulations. These positions included Commanding Officer, Executive Officer, Navigator, Communications Officer, Engineering Officer, Gunnery Officer, Commissary Officer, and First Lieutenant.²⁹ The Commanding Officer by himself has a long list of duties and responsibilities and was typically not assigned any other collateral duties. This left all of the other tasks to be performed by only two officers. This required them to multi-task at a very high level, a situation that is difficult to manage even by early 21st century standards, where highly educated officers have a myriad of automatic systems to assist them, and outright problematic in 1921. A fourth officer billet would have been immensely helpful in easing the workload. It is also known that while in port at Pearl Harbor, officers from the division's boats were called to the flagship *Chicago* to stand watches there as Officer of the Deck. For instance, Gallemore stood two officer-of the deck (OOD) watches on the *Chicago* on 26 May, after the *R-14's* return to port.³⁰ These extra watches pulled the officers of the boats away from their already assigned duties and made the problems of overwork caused by inadequate billeting even more acute. In addition, the boat was not billeted for an enlisted yeoman, a sailor specializing in typing and administrative tasks. The presence of a yeoman would have eased the administrative burden on the officers and may have prevented some of the log keeping issues.

---

²⁷ *The United States Navy: 200 Years*, Captain Edward L. Beach, USN (Ret.), 1986, page 421, 443.
²⁸ *Log Book, USS R-14, Jan. 1, 1921 to Dec. 31, 1921*, page 255.
²⁹ Derived from a table in *Seamanship, Navpers 16118, June 1944*, Chapter 7.
³⁰ *Log Book, USS Chicago and S/M Base, Jan. 1, 1921 to Dec. 31, 1921*, page 308.

4. **The Absence of Clarke.** The *R-14*'s officially assigned Commanding Officer was Lt. Vincent Arthur Clarke, Jr., the boat's only CO since her commissioning and a Navy Cross awardee from WWI. Clarke was a hot-running up-and-comer and had been recognized early on by Nimitz as someone he needed on his undermanned division staff. Several months prior to the May incident, Nimitz informally pulled Clarke to his staff as the division Engineering Officer, without relief available for the *R-14* (see Part One). The loss of the experienced and capable Clarke would have been keenly felt aboard *R-14*, compounding the difficulties brought on by the inadequate billeting described above and greatly increasing the workload of Douglas and Gallemore. In addition, the two officers had lost immediate access to an experienced mentor and capable leader and now had to handle the boat for the most part on their own. To be fair, Nimitz would not have taken this action if he did not believe that Douglas and Gallemore could handle the boat; indeed they were both very highly regarded. However, it can be said that even the wise and capable Nimitz could be blinded as to the true level of expertise of the two men by his own pressing staff needs and by their own natural confidence in themselves. Douglas and Gallemore's experience level was such that they handled the routine in-and-out training operations around Hawaii in fine fashion, and this gave Clarke and Nimitz the confidence needed to allow them to handle the search and rescue operation on their own. But they were still young and lacking the proper seasoning needed for this kind of unplanned contingency mission, and in the rushed preparations for it, this lack of seasoning became apparent. In essence, Nimitz may have unintentionally set these two officers up for failure. Twenty-twenty hindsight being what it is, it may have been a good idea to send Clarke back to the *R-14* for the duration of this important mission; surely, he could have been spared from Nimitz's staff for ten days. On the other hand, with more than half of the division's boats not capable of getting underway, perhaps Clarke couldn't be spared. Nimitz's thinking on this is not known.

5. **Underway Watch Standing.** One of the officers must always be on duty while underway as the Officer of the Deck. The absence of Clarke for this operation forced Douglas and Gallemore into a "port and starboard" OOD watch rotation, meaning each man was the other's relief. Normal watch rotation at the time was four hours on, eight hours off. This was obviously

not possible with only two men, and thus they were forced to improvise a watch schedule that would keep one of them on duty at all times but still allow adequate rest. The logs indicate that the two men varied this rotation considerably for the mission, sometimes standing four-hour watches, sometimes eight hours, and even twelve or more hours per watch. This lack of a set schedule has an enormous disturbing effect on diurnal cycles. The end effect was that the two men were constantly sleep deprived and operating on the edge of exhaustion. While this would not have had an effect on 02 May, the day they fueled the boat, it very well may have played a factor in them missing or discounting obvious signs of fuel system derangement during the days leading up to running out of fuel on the 11th.

6. **Material Condition of the Boats.** The R-class submarines were a product of the Electric Boat Company (EB) of Groton, CT. The *R-14* herself had been built by an EB subcontractor in Quincy, MA, called Bethlehem Quincy (BQ). EB was the premier civilian builder of submarines in the world and the Navy heavily relied on them. Since 1900 they had developed a near monopoly on submarine construction in the US, and in doing so, they had also developed a reputation of building boats with less-than-optimal features and construction quality.[31] The *R-14* had been in commission for over 18 months and during that time she had been run pretty hard. Opportunities for comprehensive maintenance had been lacking, and the long trip to Hawaii from California had worn all of the SUBDIV 14 boats down. In May 1921, of the division's ten boats only four were able to get underway for the *Conestoga* search and rescue mission, and even those four boats were suffering from various maladies. In interviews with two of Gallemore's grandsons, the authors confirmed that the *R-14* was in rough shape in May and was in great need of a thorough overhaul. The Pearl Harbor Navy Yard was still in an early development stage at that time, with some facilities not yet built and others still under construction. A few submarine tenders rotated in and out of Pearl Harbor and that helped with maintenance, but in general, the overall material condition of the SUBDIV 14 boats in May 1921 was not good. Constant maintenance

---

[31] *Under Pressure*, A.J. Hill, 2010, page 10.

issues strained the crew, affected the performance of the boats, and prevented adequate training.

The Aftermath

Nimitz, being the meticulous and conscientious officer that he was, would have been keenly interested in the incident and would have wanted to know the hows and whys. A submarine under his command had been hazarded at sea and Naval Regulations required him to conduct an investigation. Rear Admiral Shoemaker, the 14th Naval District commander, would have also wanted some answers. Shoemaker was the senior officer in Hawaii at the time and overall responsibility for the *Conestoga* search and rescue operation in the Hawaiian sea frontier fell to him. He had been interviewed by a reporter from the *Honolulu Star-Bulletin* on the 16th of May once it became known that the *R-14* had arrived in Hilo. He expressed confidence in the boat's imminent return and said that he did not know why the boat would have been out of fuel. Getting his name on public record would have undoubtedly made Shoemaker very interested in getting to the bottom of the issue and would have insisted on Nimitz conducting a timely investigation. The authors have no doubt that Nimitz actually did so, but in conducting research, it was determined that the National Archives had no record of any such proceedings on file, and it is not mentioned at all in E.B. Potter's highly regarded 1976 biography *Nimitz*. So, what follows is in part informed speculation on the authors' part and part inference based on known facts.

Nimitz would have begun the fact-finding immediately after the return of the *R-14* to Pearl Harbor, most likely no later than the 18th or 19th of May. He would have called into his office Clarke, Douglas, Gallemore, most likely all four of the *R-14*'s Chiefs, and a representative from the fuel facility. His adjutant and an enlisted yeoman would have also been present. Interviews of all the principals would have been conducted, and pertinent documents like the logs would have been reviewed. At the end, we are confident in saying that Nimitz would have come to many of the same conclusions that we have spelled out so far. The most difficult decision left to Nimitz at this point was what to do about it.

Nimitz would have been within his rights to recommend either Douglas or Gallemore, or both, for court-martial proceedings. That was an extreme step, and given the circumstances of the incident, there was a real chance that it would not have gone well for the two lieutenants. However, we believe that Nimitz called upon a past experience to guide him in his decision.

In 1907 as a newly commissioned ensign, Nimitz was given command of the destroyer USS *Decatur* (DD-5) at Cavite in the Philippines. At just twenty-two years of age, the move by Admiral Uriah Harris to give Nimitz command was virtually unprecedented but justifiable by Nimitz's impeccable record up to that point. Nimitz did very well with the *Decatur* until the evening of 07 July 1908. Prior to entering Batangas Harbor that evening, Nimitz failed to check the tide tables and badly overestimated the tide level. He also only used his seaman's eye to judge his position visually and failed to take the necessary bearings to verify where he was. The end result was that the *Decatur* ran aground on a mud bank. After attempts to free her failed, Nimitz and the crew calmly waited until the next morning when a local steamer came by and pulled them off. Nimitz dutifully reported the incident and was promptly relieved of command in order to stand court-martial. The subsequent trial found him guilty of "neglect of duty", but taking into account the poor state of the charts for the Batangas area and Nimitz's prior spotless record, he was sentenced only to a public reprimand by the local area commander, who decided that the proceedings themselves constituted a public reprimand and thus no further action was taken against Nimitz. He had figuratively dodged a bullet and was returned to full duty status.[32]

The benevolent result of the court-martial undoubtedly influenced Nimitz's decision regarding how to handle the *R-14* incident. He was faced with a narrow line to walk, and in the end, he navigated it brilliantly.

To begin with, and most importantly, the *R-14* and her crew had been hazarded due to neglect. With just slightly different circumstances the incident could have turned out very badly. The fact that it did not was irrelevant. Obvious mistakes had been made by the crew, mistakes that in wartime would have been fatal. Nimitz could not just let that go without some sort of action. Taking no action would have sent the entirely wrong message to the rest of the boats in the division that sloppy log keeping, inattention to detail, and failure to follow procedure would be

---

[32] *Nimitz*, E.B. Potter, 1976, page 59, 61.

tolerated and sanctioned. A message, loud and clear, needed to be sent to all of the boat's crews to tighten up their operations immediately.

To counter that, Nimitz came to realize how brilliantly the entire crew of the *R-14* had performed in recovering from the incident. Douglas and Gallemore in particular refused to give in to despair or acrimony; they came up with an innovative and novel solution, and they provided the leadership and guidance needed to get the boat and the crew back home intact. When combined with their previous unimpeachable career performance, Nimitz realized that he had two highly capable officers in front of him —ones who could have excellent careers if allowed to continue to serve. Ruining their careers with a court-marshal would not only do them a great personal disservice, it would also negatively impact the Navy as a whole.

Nimitz would have also recognized his own role in this. He had been blinded by the big picture needs of the division and the submarine base and had failed to recognize that Douglas and Gallemore, while outstanding officers, were not yet ready to fully handle the *R-14* under these conditions. By pulling Clarke to his staff without relief, he had solved one problem at his command but created another problem on the *R-14*. He had set up the two lieutenants for failure.

Tangential to the problem but not unimportant, was the fact that the incident had been picked up and reported by the news services. The coverage was actually quite favorable, portraying the crew and the Navy in a positive light. Recommending the two men for a court-martial at this point would generate some awkward questions in the press. With the Washington Naval Conference on disarmament already planned for later that year, the last thing the Navy needed was press coverage that could potentially degrade the perception of a professional Navy.

Nimitz's solution was multi-faceted and satisfied all of the competing issues. In the blue-blood atmosphere of Annapolis in the 1920s, graduates were very socially conscious, and moving up to command means that they also moved up in the all-important social rankings. Indeed, the comings and goings of military officers were routinely reported in the social columns of most major newspapers. Realizing that both Douglas and Gallemore needed further guidance before being fully ready for command, yet still needing Clarke on his staff, Nimitz got orders written to transfer Lieutenant Clifford H. Roper from command of the *R-13* (SS-90) to the *R-14*. Roper was a highly regarded and experienced CO along the same lines as Clarke. Literally walking down the pier from one boat to the next, he would take over the *R-14* until such a time as both Roper and Nimitz were satisfied that Douglas and Gallemore were ready to move up. Even though he had been the Acting Commanding Officer for some time, officially denying command to Douglas was a personal rebuke that sent the message that Nimitz wanted, without the career damaging legal proceedings on his record. The transfer of Roper to *R-14* and the denial of command to Douglas sent a message to the rest of the officers on the sub base waterfront that there were consequences to sub-par performance, and that Nimitz was not going to tolerate it. The lateral transfer of Roper, generally frowned upon in a service that promotes the concept of "move up or move out", proved to have little effect on him personally, as he went on to have a distinguished naval career, including major command billets and combat action in WWII.[33]

Nimitz realized that they had to cater to the press somewhat. Wanting to assure Douglas that he recognized that he had been put into a bad situation but had performed brilliantly, Nimitz had a Letter of Commendation drawn up for him. This was a pointed attempt by Nimitz to soften the personal blow to Douglas of not getting full command of the *R-14*, and to let him know that he still had faith in the young officer.[34]

Lastly, the authors are convinced that Nimitz and Clarke insisted that when the official logs were typed up at the end of the month that the amounts listed for fuel onboard and fuel used reflected the actual amounts that were onboard and not the amounts that the crew thought they had on 01 and 02 May. This would serve to ensure that the historical record was accurate, and it would also deflect any blame that may come their way from any subsequent investigations into the matter.

Roy Trent Gallemore came out of the incident in fine shape. His career continued in the Navy and submarines, including eventual command of the *R-15* (SS-92). In the mid 1920s he transferred his commission to the Naval Reserve and returned home to Bartow, Florida, to help his recently widowed mother publish the *Polk County Record*. He remained in the Naval Reserve and was called back to active duty in 1940. Nimitz had retained a favorable opinion of Gallemore in the years

---

[33] Roper commanded the heavy cruiser *Chicago* and received the Navy Cross for his "extraordinary heroism" after she was torpedoed at the Battle of Tassafaronga 30 November 1942.

[34] *R-14 Underway, Under Sail*, Naval History Magazine, August 2004 issue, LCDR Robert G. Douglas, USN (Ret.), page 61.

since the incident. In the summer of 1945 Gallemore was recuperating from an illness at a naval hospital in Hawaii. While out for a stroll in his robe and pajamas, Roy passed the five-star Fleet Admiral Nimitz, who paused and greeted him by asking, "Roy! How are you doing and how is your wife?"[35] For a prestigious Admiral like Nimitz to pause and take the time to acknowledge and inquire about an officer he knew from twenty years prior was taken by Gallemore as a sincere compliment. At the war's conclusion, Gallemore was stationed in the Micronesian islands where he developed a deep affection for the people and their culture. In 1954 he retired from the Navy Reserve and accepted a position with the Department of the Interior. He returned to Micronesia, which included former battlefields in the Northern Marianas and Caroline Islands, and he faithfully served the US government and the local population there for the next ten years. He was instrumental in the process of transitioning the Trust Territory of the Pacific Islands to the fully independent Federated States of Micronesia. He fully retired in 1965 and returned to Bartow, where he passed away in 1977.

Alexander Dean Douglas had a long and varied career. The *R-14* incident had little discernible impact because by 1925 he was back in Hawaii to officially command the *R-3* (SS-80). He later commanded the larger and more capable *S-44* (SS-155) and *S-38* (SS-143). He also conducted shore duty tours in Portland, OR, and Washington DC. By 1938 he was the Executive Officer of the submarine tender *Holland* (AS-3), and in 1941, he was the first Commanding Officer of the submarine tender *Fulton* (AS-11) as a full Captain. In 1942 he had moved up further, serving as a convoy commander for troop convoys to North Africa. He retired from the Navy in 1947 and lived a peaceful life until his death in 1989.

R-14's official Commanding Officer during the incident, Lieutenant Vincent A. Clarke, Jr. had a very interesting but unfortunately short career. After being awarded the Navy Cross for his persistent and aggressive command of the submarine *L-10* (SS-50) during WWI, Clarke had earned the reputation of a highly capable and outstanding officer. He performed admirably on Nimitz's staff at Submarine Division 14 and continued his excellent service in the submarine community until 1925. In that year, looking for a new way to serve, he asked for and was approved for a transfer to Naval Aviation. After earning his wings of gold, he was accepted for airship duty and trained in balloons and non-rigid blimps. As a USN representative he made the second voyage across the Atlantic on the German rigid

---

[35] Emails to authors from Bruce Gallemore dated 28 May 2021, and 11 August 2021.

airship *Graf Zeppelin* in the summer of 1929. On that voyage he made friends with famed polar explorer Sir Hubert Wilkins, who later made an attempt to reach the North Pole via submarine. By May 1930, he was in command of the rigid airship USS *Los Angeles* (ZR-3). In the summer of 1932, he transferred to the San Francisco Navy Yard. Shortly thereafter he became ill and was hospitalized. Blood poisoning caused his health to rapidly deteriorate. He died peacefully at the Naval Hospital there on 10 August 1932. He was survived by his wife Charlotte and one daughter.

The *R-14* herself led a mundane but useful life after the sailing incident. She continued to run training operations out of Pearl Harbor until December 1930, when she departed the islands for the last time and headed east. The boat and her crew arrived at the submarine base in New London, CT, in February 1931, and for the next ten years, they conducted training missions for students at the Submarine School. In 1939 she was featured in a *Life* magazine article highlighting life aboard a submarine. In the summer of 1941, as war loomed, the boat shifted homeports to Naval Station Key West, FL. *R-14* ran training missions in the Straits of Florida, the Gulf of Mexico, and the Yucatan Channel for the Navy's Sound School. She also ran anti U-boat patrols in those areas, although none were ever sighted or attacked. By the spring of 1945 the 25-year-old *R-14* was thoroughly worn out and with scores of brand-new fleet submarines now in the fleet the old workhorse was at the end of her days. The Navy decommissioned her at the Philadelphia Navy Yard on 07 May 1945. The hulk lingered there until 1946, when *R-14* finally and unceremoniously succumbed to the ravages of time and the scrapper's torch. The submarine that provided lessons to her crew and the Navy by finding a good and favorable wind now belonged to history.

LESSONS LEARNED

It is often said in the 21st century Navy that Navy Regulations and procedures are written in blood. The inference is that the enduring lessons are unfortunately learned the hard way. While thankfully no one was killed or injured in this incident and no equipment was lost or even damaged, there are still lessons that can be applied to modern operations; because as Winston Churchill put it, "Those that fail to learn from history are doomed to repeat it."

First, the necessity of maintaining a proper log was dramatically emphasized here. It is distinctly possible that a transposed digit in fuel usage or the absence of one or two numbers was the root cause of running out of fuel. All sailors, from the newest Fireman/Seaman up to the Commanding Officer must be thoroughly indoctrinated with the indispensability of proper and accurate logs. Not only will small errors in logs grow into bigger errors later, it also goes a long way toward demonstrating professionalism.

Procedural compliance was just as important in 1921 as it is now. Procedures are there for a reason. They will assist in reducing the effect of human nature, and they will make the organization more efficient, safe, and mission effective. Failure to follow procedure in this case gave us an interesting historical footnote to debate. In wartime, the result would have been tragic. On the other hand, it is indeed ironic that Douglas and Gallemore saved the boat with a technique for which there was no procedure. That in itself is a corollary lesson. Procedural compliance need not paralyze a sailor's actions when innovative, outside-the-box thinking becomes imperative.

Related to procedural compliance is the idea that "qualified does not equal proficient". It is distinctly possible that the *R-14* ran out of fuel because one or more of her qualified crewmen missed signs of fuel system derangement because of a lack of proficiency in the operation of the system. It has also been shown that both Douglas and Gallemore, while fine and highly capable officers, were not yet ready to command under these conditions. There is a tendency to believe that once the watch station qualification procedure is completed and signed off by proper authority, the sailor is instantly proficient and experienced. Those two qualities *only come with time and proper mentoring.* The members of the crew that are truly proficient, such as the senior officers, chiefs, and senior petty officers, must continue to monitor newly qualified personnel to ensure that the training took hold, and that procedures are being followed. Human nature dictates that "qualified" personnel, who have a desire to validate the trust that has been placed in them, will be loath to admit that they are unclear on an issue or not fully proficient. Follow-up mentoring and training will ensure that the training sets in properly.[36]

Aboard modern USN warships there is a watch position called "Fuel King." This crewmember is thoroughly trained in the operation of the fuel system, and when fuel is taken on board or moved from tank to tank, the Fuel King is the person in charge. This establishes a clear line of responsibility to the Engineering Officer and up to the Commanding Officer. It eliminates the old saw that says, "If everyone is in charge, then no one is." While the authors have yet to determine the exact origin of the watch station, we strongly believe that the institutional memory of the *R-14* incident may have been the nexus for the creation of the Fuel King position in the USN.[37]

Chester Nimitz's handling of the situation and its aftermath was a model of even-handed fairness. Yes, mistakes had been made and a warship had been unduly hazarded, but he took the time to consider the mitigating factors and the circumstances involved. In a moment of self-reflection, he also saw that his own actions played a part in the mess. He recognized the qualities of Douglas and Gallemore and knew that when all things were considered, these two men were outstanding officers that could have brilliant careers in the Navy if allowed to do so. He deftly walked the line between discipline and fairness and the results are unimpeachable. The authors have seen a tendency in today's Navy to conduct witch hunts when mistakes are made, with a level of disregard for circumstances and mitigating factors. It is the old monster of the Zero-Defect Mentality, and it has an extremely debilitating effect on crew morale.[38] We consider this to be one of the strongest take-aways from this incident. Mistakes are okay under certain

---

[36] *A Report on the Fighting Culture of the United States Navy Surface Fleet,* Schmidle & Montgomery, 2021, page 14. https://www.cotton.senate.gov/imo/media/doc/navy_report.pdf

[37] The earliest reference to "oil king" we could find online was *Our Navy, the Standard Publication of the U.S. Navy,* page 26. 1920. https://books.google.com/books/content?id=FIM9AQAA-MAAJ&pg=RA10-PA26&img=1&zoom=3&hl=en&bul=1&sig=ACfU3U2ir-SOgY9EjlYb_IWsC0CFqGy9ekA&ci=366%2C580%2C282%2C58&edge=0

[38] *Report on the Fighting Culture...,* page 9.

conditions, and oftentimes, can be completely forgiven because they can be one of the most powerful learning experiences a person can have. Recognize the inherent qualities of sailors, and if they can be saved, do the utmost to save them because they are the future of the Navy.

Optimal manning of warships is one of the most difficult tasks that faces any navy. Having too many sailors aboard ship is cost-prohibitive and creates management issues for the chiefs and officers. With too few sailors a breeding ground is created for inefficiency, overwork, low morale, and dangerous operating conditions. There is admittedly a fine line to walk, but failure to do so can have serious consequences. The *R-14* clearly could have benefited from not only an enlisted yeoman, but from at least one more officer billet. Pulling Clarke off the boat for temporary duty at the division was, in hindsight, a bad decision that exacerbated an already tenuous manning problem. Today's USN struggles every day with manning issues, trying to mitigate economic and technological factors. The *R-14* incident is a reminder of the consequences of not getting it right.

Maintenance of warships is a never-ending task. If not done completely and efficiently it will have a serious deleterious effect on mission capability. Sixty percent of the SUBDIV 14 boats were unable to get underway for a life-and-death search and rescue operation due to deferred or incomplete maintenance, and those that did, like *R-14*, were struggling with seaworthiness. Maintenance *must be a priority* for the USN. That was true in 1921, and it is still true 100 years later.[39]

Finally, the United States Navy exists solely, when taken to its core mission, to seek out and destroy those who would do this nation harm. The USN of 1921 had lost touch with that purpose, wrapped up in the euphoria of the aftermath of "The War to End All Wars" and the false promise of broad-based disarmament. Not knowing exactly what to train for will result in training that is at best ineffective. A military service should not train to fight the last war, and it can't train to fight the next one unless it has a clear vision of what the next war will be. Establish a strategic vision and provide the country's military forces with the resources necessary to train to that vision. Anything less will result in pernicious routine, malaise, and potential tragedy.

---

[39] Ibid, page 16.

Postscript: The Fate of the USS *Conestoga* (AT-54)

It was unknown at the time, but the warships that sallied forth from Pearl Harbor in May 1921, to search for the *Conestoga* in Hawaiian waters never had the slightest chance of finding her. The *Conestoga*'s exact fate remained a mystery for ninety-four years.

She got underway from the Mare Island Navy Yard on 25 March 1921, bound for American Samoa with a transient stop in Hawaii, a laden coal barge in tow. Shortly after departing San Francisco Bay, she sailed into a fierce gale. Strong winds and heavy seas buffeted the ship. Her Commanding Officer, Lieutenant Ernest Larkin Jones, sought temporary shelter in the lee of a cove on South Farallon Island, in the Farallon Island chain just thirty miles from the Golden Gate. They didn't make it. Heavily battered by the mountainous seas, the *Conestoga* sank with all hands just three miles from the cove. There is a distinct possibility that she was dragged down by the coal barge she was towing. In essence she had dipeared without a trace. Communications foul-ups and missed clues caused the Navy to lose track of her. Weeks passed until an alarm was finally raised. The Navy made an assumption that the ship was much farther west; thus, the ultimately futile search that was made in Hawaiian waters. On 30 June 1921, all further attempts to find her were called off and the *Conestoga* was officially declared lost with all hands, cause and location unknown.

In perhaps the luckiest shipwreck find of the century, her wreck was stumbled across in 2009 by a National Oceanic and Atmospheric Administration (NOAA) expedition that was on a general survey of the Farallon Islands looking to document other known wrecks in the area. At first unsure of what they were looking at, the NOAA team was intrigued by her unique silhouette and came back for a follow-up in 2014. Photographic and video evidence was studied and the team, stunned by the facts, concluded that they had found the grave of the *Conestoga*.[40] Confirmed by the Navy in 2015, this 94-year-old mystery has been laid to rest and

---

[40] Smithsonianmag.com, March 23, 2016, author Suzy Khimm

the families of the missing sailors now know the full story of their loved ones. Rest in peace, shipmates.

Figure 45. The last photo taken of the entire crew of the USS *Conestoga* (AT-54). This photo was taken in March 1921 just prior to her departure from the Mare Island Navy Yard in Vallejo, CA. The Commanding Officer, Lt. Ernest L. Jones, is in the center of the front row, wearing the dress blues with the high collar. Less than a month after this photo was taken, all of these men disappeared into the Pacific Ocean. *R-14* was among the vessels sent to search for them. NHHC Photo NH71503 via Navsource.org.

Figure 46. An artist's rendition of the last moments of the *Conestoga* and her crew. She was a small boat in a big lonely sea. Courtesy Daniel Frka and the Russ Matthews Collection. Used with permission via the Navy Art Collection, Naval History and Heritage Command.

Figure 47. Stern view of the shipwreck of USS *Conestoga* (AT-54) in the Greater Farallones National Marine Sanctuary. The wreck is colonized with white plumose sea anemones. Photo courtesy Robert Hurst via Navsource.org / US Navy photo # 151001-N-ZZ999-304 Pacific Ocean (March 1, 2016), courtesy of NOAA.

Appendix A. Sailing List, USS *R-14* (SS-91), May 1921

Last Name	First Name	Rate/Rank
Black	Leland C.	Seaman 2nd class
Bridges	Winfield E.	Gunner's Mate 1st class
Cameron	David W.	Fireman 1st class
Clarke	Vincent A. Jr.	Lieutenant (Commanding Officer)
Clay	William S.	Ships Cook 1st class
Clendenny	Jesse L.	Fireman 3rd class
Dew	John W.	Quartermaster 2nd class
Dorsey	John J.	Gunner's Mate 1st class
Douglas	Alexander D.	Lieutenant (Acting Commanding Officer)
Dunham	George E.	Fireman 1st class
Emerline	Roy P.	Engineman 1st class
Field	Valoris E.	Electrician 2nd class (General)
Foren	Percy J.	Electrician 3rd class (General)
Gallemore	Roy T.	Lieutenant
Gottlieb	?	(unknown)
Graham	Wallace J.	Chief Machinist Mate
Hearne	Joseph H.	Chief Electrician (General)
Kaessner	Walter D.	Machinist Mate 1st class
Kruskowski	Leo P.	Seaman 1st class
LaFoy	Hansell H.	Electrician 3rd class
McGlencey	William	Gunner's Mate 1st class (General)
McNamara	Hugh	Machinist Mate 1st class
Riggs	Willie K.	Fireman 1st class

Robinson	Revie O.	Fireman 3rd class
Roper	Clifford H.	Lieutenant (Relieving Commanding Officer)
Ross	Albert	Fireman 2nd class
Ruchas	Joseph S.	Gunners Mate 2nd class (General)
Russell	James C.	Seaman 1st class
Skreypczak	Albert	Seaman 2nd class
Stakely	William A.	Electrician 3rd class (General)
Suess	Raymond R.	Seaman 1st class
Sullivan	Patrick J.	Fireman 2nd class
Verano	Lorenzo	Mess Attendant 2nd class
Waldron	Raymond W.	Electrician 1st class (Radio)
Wilde	Sidney W.	Chief Gunners Mate (Torpedo)
Wilkinson	Henry D.	Seaman 1st class
Woodworth	Harry E.	Chief Gunners Mate (Torpedo)
Wrenn	Dennis P.	Machinist Mate 1st class

Appendix B. A Short History of PigBoats.COM

In the late 1990's Ric Hedman had discovered eBay and out of curiosity and a long-standing fascination with submarine history he did a search for [submarines] and discovered a multitude of images, most of which didn't really catch his attention. He did see a number of images of older submarines and they began to intrigue him. He came across a small personal photo album with pictures of several K-class submarines. Making a bid he eventually won it. When the album arrived it was discovered that the photos were quite small so Ric electronically scanned them so that he could enlarge them to see better detail.

Ric was just learning about web page construction at the time so he placed the images all on one page and uploaded it to the web. He posted a link to the photos for his fellow sub sailors on a bulletin board site. That was the beginning of what was to first become a web page called "Through the Looking Glass: A Photographic Essay of U.S. Submarines, 1900-1940." In 2000 a fellow submariner by the name of Dave Johnston emailed Ric to comment on a particular photograph and some information that was in the background of the picture. That lone email started off a twenty year collaboration and a strong friendship. Both men had an abiding interest in submarine history and they shared a strong desire to get it right.

In 2005 Ric purchased the internet domain "PigBoats.COM" and transferred all the code to there and retired the old domain. In 2019 Ric and Dave became full partners in the site and have since collaborated on several published articles on submarine history. The photographic resources of the site have caught the attention of numerous authors, and Ric and Dave have consulted with these authors on their projects, providing photographs and technical reviews. PigBoats.COM continues today as one of the premier sites on the web concerning this early period of USN submarine history.

BIBLIOGRAPHY

OFFICIAL U.S. NAVY DOCUMENTS

Log Book, U.S.S. R-14, Jan. 1, 1921 to Dec. 31,1921, pp. 1-3 plus continuances, 256-329.

Log Book, U.S.S. Chicago and *S/M Base*, Jan 1.1921 to Dec, 31, 1921, pp. 308.

Log Book, U.S.S. R-13, Jan. 1, 1921 to Dec. 31, 1921, pp. 304.

Log Book, U.S.S. R-12, Jan. 1, 1921 to Dec. 31, 1921, pp. 288-293.

Log Book, U.S.S. Eagle #14, Jan 1. 1921 to Dec. 31, 1921, pp. 249-250.

BOOKS

U.S. Submarines Through 1945: An Illustrated Design History, Norman Friedman, Naval Institute Press, 1995, ISBN: 1-55750-263-3.

US Submarines 1900-35, Jim Christley, Osprey Publishing Ltd., 2011, ISBN: 978-1-84908-185-6.

MAGAZINE ARTICLES AND MONOGRAPHS

"R-14 Under Way, Under Sail", Robert G. Douglas, *Naval History Magazine*, August, 2004.

"The Navy Finds A Way", O.H. Wright, *Polk County Historical Quarterly*, Volume 19, Number 1, June, 1992.

Submarine Under Sail, H.D. Wilkinson, publisher and date unknown.

NEWSPAPER ARTICLES

"Officials Give Up Conestoga, Naval Tug, As Lost", *The New York Times*, June 22, 1921.

"Navy Tug Missing At Sea", *The Washington Post*, May 4, 1921.

"Submarine Reaches Port Under Sails", *The Duluth Herald*, May 17, 1921.

"Disabled Sub Uses Sails", *The Manchester Democrat*, July 13, 1921

INDEX

Baker, Darryl	31, 32, 37, 38, 40, 41, 43, 54, 58
batteries	15, 31, 32, 33, 34, 36, 37, 40, 43, 44, 50, 51, 54, 57, 59, 61, 65, 66, 69
Bethlehem Quincy	xix
Bridges, Winfield E., Gunner's Mate 1st class	9
Cape Kumukahi	60, 61
Christley, Jim	xvii, 13, 15, 39, 59, 64, 76, 77, 80, 110
Clarke, Vincent A., Lieutenant and Commanding Officer R-14	3, 6, 73, 78, 81, 82, 87, 90, 93, 95, 96, 97, 101
Douglas, Alexander Dean, Lieutenant USN	xii, xvii, 2 3, 5, 8, 19, 24, 26, 27, 33, 34, 47, 49, 50, 51, 52, 53, 56, 59, 60, 61, 63, 64, 65, 66, 73, 81, 82, 86, 87, 90, 93, 94, 95, 96, 97, 99, 100, 110
Electric Boat (EB)	xiv, 13, 80, 91
Emerline, Roy P., Engineman 1st class	35, 49, 73
engines	ix, 2, 15, 19, 21, 25, 35, 36, 44, 45, 47, 51, 52, 59, 60, 66, 69, 77, 80, 82, 84
Jones, Ernest Larkin, Lieutenant	102
Ford Island	1, 19, 23
Ford, Henry	14, 15, 18
Gallemore, Charlotte	98
Gallemore Eliot, Katie	xvi, 28, 68
Gallemore, Roy Trent, Lieutenant USN	xvi, xvii, 24, 25, 26, 27, 28, 36, 47, 49, 50, 52, 53, 59, 60, 65, 68, 73, 74, 81, 82, 84, 86, 87, 89, 90, 91, 93, 95, 96, 97, 98, 99
Hearne, Joseph H., Chief Electrician (General)	52, 59, 65, 68, 69
Hilo	xxi, 50, 58, 59, 60, 61, 62, 65, 67, 68, 69, 73, 80, 82, 93
Holland, John P.	13, 84
Kuahua	2, 10
logs and Log Book,	xii, xvii, 1, 14, 15, 16, 20, 21, 36, 52, 57, 59, 60, 61, 62, 65, 73, 78, 79, 80, 81, 82, 83, 84, 85, 86, 87, 89, 91, 93, 94, 96, 99
masts	57, 64, 65
Matson Line	36, 65
McNamara, Hugh (Machinist Mate 1st class)	3, 4, 19, 49, 107
Nimitz, Admiral Chester W.	2, 3, 14, 18, 21, 24, 62, 66, 73, 83, 86, 90, 93, 94, 95, 96, 97, 100

Pearl Harbor	iii, 1, 2, 10, 11, 14, 19, 22, 23, 30, 66, 67, 68, 69, 75, 80, 83, 89, 91, 93, 98
Potter, E. B.	2, 93, 94
R-class submarines	xvii, 2, 12, 13, 15, 15, 40, 59, 61, 80, 89, 91
Roper, Clifford H.	73, 95, 96
Ruchas, Joseph, Gunner's Mate 1st class	68, 108
S-class submarines	xvi, 13, 98
sails	53, 56, 60, 61, 64, 65
Shoemaker, William, Rear Admiral	14, 93
Submarine Base Pearl Harbor	iii, 2, 11
Suess Family and Suess Family Collection	7, 8, 9, 29, 39, 42, 55, 63, 64, 67, 69, 75
Suess, Raymond, Seaman 1st class	xvii, 7, 8, 9, 29, 42, 55, 63, 64, 67, 69, 75
USS Conestoga	iv, 7, 14, 17, 25, 34, 35, 81, 91, 93, 102, 104, 105, 106, 110, iv, 14, 17, 104, 106
USS Decatur	94
USS R-12	12, 14, 62, 66, 67, 73, 82, 110; see also R-class submarines
Vallejo Naval & Historical Museum	31, 32, 38, 40, 41, 43, 54, 58
Waipio	22
Waldron, Raymond W., Electrician 1st class (Radio)	52, 56, 61
Wilkinson, Henry D., Seaman 1st class	56, 65, 68, 110
Woodworth, Harry, Chief Gunner's Mate (Torpedo)	xvii, 3, 8, 19, 50, 51, 52, 53, 56, 59, 60, 65